"Nietzsche's Philosophy of Religion: A destructive tool towards a constructive outlook"

Ismita Pandey

TABLE OF CONTENTS

SL. No.	Chapter	Pg. No.
	Acknowledgement	i-ii
Chapter I	Nietzsche as a philosopher	1-40
	1.1 New order of philosophers	
	1.2 "A Disciple of philosopher Dionysus"	
	1.3 Notion of religion as a subject matter of philosophical enquiry	
Chapter II	Concept of religion and its various aspects	41-97
	2.1 The Initial men and their gods.	
	2.2 The prophetic religions.	
	2.3 Indian religions, Confucianism and Taoism.	
	2.4 The collapse of God	
Chapter III	Existential approach towards religion	98-139
	3.1 Theist/Christian existentialism	
	3.2 Kierkegaard and Nietzsche	
	3.3 Sartre and Camus	
Chapter IV	A critical analysis of Nietzsche's Repudiations	140-170
	4.1 "Pure spirit" or "pure stupidity"	
	4.2 The gadfly	
Chapter V	Concluding Nietzsche's philosophy of religion: A destructive tool towards a constructive outlook.	171-179

chapter 1

Nietzsche as a philosopher

Friedrich Nietzsche is a name well known for his scholarly and intellectual remarks over various aspects of everyday human life; let it be culture, religion or morality. He is quoted all over the word by rebellious and unconventional minds. He was an extraordinary thinker and has written about almost every field, but whether to consider him as a philosopher or not is still a stubject under debate. There have been differences between the scholars regarding the matter. Gilles Deleuze, an eminent scholar presents the dilemma as follows;

"Nietzsche's posthumous fate is burdened by two ambiguities, was his thought a fore-runner of fascist thinking? And was his thought itself really philosophy or was it an over-violent poetry made up of capricious aphorisms and pathological fragments?" (Deleuze)[1]

Not only the fascist movement or anti-Semitism[2] Nietzsche is associated with many 'isms' of his time, yet, he belongs to none. Due to his sister, Frau Forster Nietzsche's arbitrary use of his unpublished materials and drafts, and also because of Nietzsche's distinctly reckless style of writing, soon after his death, he gained an image of a thinker who glorifies cruelty and supports wars. In a foreword to Walter Kaufmann's Nietzsche, (4th ed.) Alexander Nehamas gives a picture of this situation-

"Nietzsche was now seen as a philosopher of heartless cruelty, a thinker in harmony with Nazi ideology who according to the Harvard

historian 'Crane Brinton', "Damned democracy, pacifism, individualism,
Christianity, humanitarianism [and] praised authority, racial purity, the
warrior spirit and practice, the stern life and great health" (kaufmann)[3]

Gradually this image got dissolved by the efforts of Nietzsche
scholars like Walter Kaufmann, who gave his heart and soul to prove that
Nietzsche was not at all interested in Nazi of fascist or any kind of
national or anti-national politics. Kaufmann describes Nietzsche as *"an*
anti-political individual who seeks self-perfection." Contemporary
academic world is continuously trying to understand Nietzsche and frame
his ideas, but every attempt to define him would be one-sided, incomplete
and unfair, as *"Nietzsche was not a member of, and cannot be claimed by,*
any school or movement, He offered fascinating ideas and theories, but
he also taught "the courage for an attack on one's own convictions""
(kaufmann 423)[4]

Nietzsche was not concerned about pure race, German nationality
or anti-Semitism, what he was concerned about is this world we live in
and further growth of us homo-sapiens, our basic instincts, say, creativity,
art and culture. He dreamt about a future where man will evolve to a new
version, which will be far better physically, mentally, psychologically and
intellectually than today's man. This dream cannot be achieved by a
tendency to follow what is already given, a tendency to believe what is
told, a tendency to belong to the masses. This tendency is the biggest
hindrance for mankind. Very common examples of this disaster are

children who are converted from a whole new individual full of possibilities to a replica of their parents and society.

"Involuntarily, parents turn children into something similar to themselves – they call that "education" .Deep in her heart, no mother doubts that the child she has borne is her property; no father contests his own right to subject it to his concepts and valuations. Indeed, formerly it seemed fair for fathers (among the ancient Germans, for example) to decide on the life or death of the new-born as they saw fit. And like the father, teachers, classes, priests, and princes still see, even today, in every new human being an unproblematic opportunity for another possession." (F. Nietzsche 107-108)[5]

And that is the reason why he hates the traditional education system, religion, morality, state and even democracy. Because all of these believe that the welfare of individual is in being one with the community, in belonging to the mass. The more precise a copy one becomes of the society around, the more respected and educated one is considered to be. According to Nietzsche there have always been few distinguished, exceptional, marvellous beings, which by their extraordinary capabilities raise the graph of man for e.g. Caesar, Frederick II, Shakespeare, Napoleon, Goethe and more. These are the kind of men who bear the burden of elevation of human life. And the other men, the common men, he considers them to be *"a mediocre species of men"*. In aphorism 228, Beyond Good and Evil, chapter 7, 'Our virtues' he clearly rejects the idea of 'general utility' or the "the happiness of the greatest number"[6], by saying that this utilitarian theory is not at all practical, as, he says, "general welfare" is no ideal, no goal, no notion that can be at all grasped, but is only a nostrum, that what is fair to one may not be fair to another, further he says that man and man are different, he believes few men to be higher than others ,and so propounding equal morals for every man will not be fair for men of higher rank, as they deserve better or different moral.

On these grounds, scholars like Julian Young, believe him to be an "Aristocratic individualist"-

"A second way in which Nietzsche is interpreted as an 'individualist'- 'an elitist' or 'aristocratic individualist'- admits, unlike the first, that Nietzsche is crucially concerned with the culture, with 'cultural greatness', But it reduces this to individualism by reading him as holding that cultural greatness consists, not in some characteristic of society as a whole, but simply in the existence of few 'excellent persons' or 'higher types' such as Beethovan or Goethe." (Young 3)[7]

This inclination towards 'higher type of men' gave him a sort of negative reputation which was uncalled for. It may be said that Nietzsche has somehow failed to express what he thinks due to his vague style. Kaufmann points towards it as follows –

"He goes out of his way to emphasize that "great things" must be "fought" for and that it take courage to win independence, for individuals as well as nations- and he fails to place equal emphasis on the point, no less important for any real understanding of his philosophy,

that, "Thoughts that come with dove's feet guide the world (z II 22 and EH-V4) and "the greatest events"- those are not our loudest but our stillest hours"(z II 18). Some great things may have issued from wars; but 'the greatest events' are experiences of those stillest hours when we are creative, absorbed and heedless of society." (kaufmann 413)[8]

His vagueness in manner of presenting his ideas and lack of system is not some kind of ignorance or carelessness on his part; instead, not having a systematic philosophy is a well thought decision based on rational reasons. He says in Twilight of the Idols-

"The will to a system in a philosopher, morally speaking, is a subtle corruption, a disease of character." Due to this unsystematic approach, it is a rigorous task to understand his philosophy as a whole. All we have are aphorisms which cover almost every aspect of human intellectual possibilities. These aphorisms are sometimes related to one-another and sometimes they appear out of nowhere. Sometimes they even seem to contradict each other. Let's take an example from "Thus Spoke Zarathustra", which is considered to be his one of the most systematic works.

In Zarathustra's prologue, aphorism 3, Zarathustra says to people;

"Once the sin against God was the greatest sin, but God died, and these sinners died with him." (F. Nietzsche, Thus Spoke Zarathustra 13)[9]

While in the 7th chapter "Reading and writing", he says;

"Now I am light, now I fly, now I see myself beneath myself, now a god dances through me." (F. Nietzsche, Thus Spoke Zarathustra 41)[10]

Here the contradiction in the use of term "God" in the both instances is obvious, unless one dives deep into the pool of Nietzsche's metaphorical, indirect, satirical methods of writing. When we do so, we find out that the term 'God' in first instance with G capital is a satirical notion or the traditional, biblical 'God' who belonged to the authority of 'church', while in the second instance, 'god' with a small g refers to the height of Nietzsche's own personal, spiritual elevation, raised above the common level of mankind. A stature to which man himself can reach someday.

His writings, though unsystematic but rich in poetic articulation of sentences captivates the readers mind at first reading, but when the reader tries to decode the central idea of the paragraph, he often gets baffled amidst the playful words, for eg. Aphorism 29 Maxim and Arrows, Twilight of Idols-

"How much conscience has had to chew on in the past! And what excellent teeth it had! And today- what is lacking? A dentist's question."

Or

Aphorism 44, same as above-

"The formula of my happiness, a Yes, a No, a straight line, a goal."

Due to this many scholars believe that Nietzsche's writings may evoke emotions, but they are incapable of providing any productive philosophy. R. J. Hollingdale's opinion about the matter seems important enough to mention :–

"Other philosophers have written poetry and other poets have philosophized, but only in Plato have intellectual and artistic ability been combined at so high a level as they were in Nietzsche. Yet this double gift has injured his reputation as a philosopher, so that it may still be necessary to insist that he was a philosopher, and not a poet and aphorist with a few fixed ideas. His memorability has worked against him: short passages stay in mind but divorced from their context and for that reason sometimes nearly meaningless or capable of being seriously misunderstood. His temperament was that of an artist and for that reason his philosophical writings are impure, in the sense that they mingle reason and sensibility, logic and rhetoric, and sometimes Dichtung and Wahrheit, in a way that baffles the orderly mind which seeks to discover 'what Nietzsche means'." (R.J.Hollindale 15)[11]

He himself was able to see that his first book "The birth of tragedy" was not remotely a well stated book of philosophy or philology, despite it was random expression of a wayward mind. As he says in his second (later) preface of '*The birth of Tragedy*' written in 1886-

"To say it once more, today I find it an impossible book. I consider it badly written, ponderous, embarrassing, image-mad, image-confused, sentimental, in places saccharine to the point of effeminacy, uneven in tempo, without the will to logical cleanliness, very convinced and therefore disdainful of proof, mistrustful even of the propriety of proof, a

book for initiates...an arrogant and rhapsodic book" (F. Nietzsche, The Birth of Tragedy and The Case of Wagner 19)[12]

Although he was not a systematic philosopher as the academic world expected of him and he never felt the obligation to become one, still, as he gradually matured as a thinker, he achieved an exceptional place in the philosophical world as an unmatched critique of the misleading beliefs of philosophers and their way of philosophising things

"Let me be pardoned, an old philologist who cannot desist from the mischief of putting his finger on bad modes of Interpretation." (F. Nietzsche 30)[13]

He doubts and raises question, he examines every presupposition and demands the same from everyone who calls himself a man of intellect. He presents uncustomary ideas and atypical concepts. He plays easily with contentious beliefs and argues against piety. Nietzsche certainly is not the philosopher in the conventional sense; rather he is one of those who provide intellectual minds a whole new dimension of non-conventional philosophy to think about. He belongs to one of those "New order of philosophers".

1.1 New order of philosophers :

Knowledge of higher intellectual value always discomforts common people. A philosopher needs to think disregarding the mob, because what pleases common people is always of common value. The quality Nietzsche is seeking in the **new order of philosophers** is a 'Free Spirit'. He must not be bound to anything, any ideologies, faith or moral, as Nietzsche says –

"... assuming first of all that the concept "philosopher" is not restricted to the philosopher who writes books- or make books of his philosophy.

A final trait for the image of the free-spirited philosopher is contributed by Stendhal, whom, considering German taste, I do not want to fail to stress- for he goes against the German taste. "pour être bon philosophe", says this last great psychologist, "il faut être sec, clair, sans illusion. Un banquier, qui a fait fortune, a une partie du caractère requis pour fair des découvertes en philosophie, cest-à-dire pour voir clair dans ce qui est."[1] (F. Nietzsche 50)[14]

Philosophers in general seem to be so much in need of **absolute knowledge, immediate certainty,** of a **thing-in-itself,** that they are ready to refuse what they feel, sense and perceive. They are so much afraid of non-existence, death, fragility, that they seek refuse in imaginary concepts of things that will exist forever, like an "immortal soul" or a "God" or "Supreme power", and this they call reality, because it will not

---

[1] "To be a good philosopher, one must be dry, clear, without illusion. A banker who has made a fortune has one character trait that is needed for making discoveries in philosophy, that is to say, for seeing clearly into what is." – Aphorism 39, pg 50, The Free spirit, Beyond Good and Evil.

change or decay or degrade (of course! It will not, because it is imaginary, like all perfections are), and so call everything else "appearance". Because it's harsh to accept that their life might have no meaning at all, that when they die, they just cease to exist, nothing remains, they will just be ash and soil, and after a much longer span of time, that too will not remain as the Earth and the whole solar-system will cease to exist. They are all hell-bent to create a whole other world, an after-life and an immortal soul because they fear oblivion, but to quote "Hazel Grace", a character from John Green's novel, "The Fault in our Stars", oblivion is inevitable,

"There will come a time, when all of us are dead. All of us. There will come a time when there are no human beings remaining to remember that anyone ever existed or that our species ever did anything. There will be no one to remember Aristotle or Cleopatra, let alone you. Everything that we did or build and wrote and thought and discovered will be forgotten and all of this will have been for a naught. May be that time is coming soon and may be its millions of years away, but even if we survive the collapse of our sun, we will not survive forever. There was a time before organisms and there will be a time after. And if the inevitability of human oblivion worries you, I encourage you to ignore it." (Green)[15]

The beauty of life lies in living it with the awareness of its momentariness, taking responsibilities of our own actions and emotions, keep on creating art, music and cultures and keep looking at truth right into its eyes.

Nietzsche expects from the new philosophers to challenge **thing-in-itself, immediate certainty, absolute knowledge** and every such theory that is superficial and beyond man's reach. According to Nietzsche these ideas involve a "contradicto-in-adjecto" i.e. contradiction between noun and adjective. Referring Descartes **cogito-ergo-sum**, he says –

"...the philosopher must say to himself: when I analyze the process that is expressed in the sentence "I think", I find a whole series of daring assertations that would be difficult, perhaps impossible, to prove; for example that it is I who think that there must necessarily be something that thinks, that thinking is an activity and operation on the part of the being who is thought of as a cause, that there is an "ego" and finally, that it is already determined what it is to be designated by thinking- that I know what thinking is. For if I had not already decided within myself what it is, by what standard could I determine whether that which is just happening is not perhaps "willing" or "feeling"? In short the assertion "I think" assumes that I compare my state at the present moment with other states of myself which I know, in order to determine what it is; on account of this retrospective connection with further "knowledge" it has, at any rate, no "immediate certainty" for me.

In place of "immediate certainty" in which the people may believe in the case at hand, the philosopher thus finds a series of metaphysical questions presented to him, truly searching questions of the intellect; to wit: "from where do I get the concept of thinking? Why do I believe in cause and effect? What gives me the right to speak of an ego, and even of an ego as cause and finally of an ego as cause of thought?" whoever ventures to answer these metaphysical questions at once by an appeal to a sort of intuitive perception, like a person who says, " I think, and know that this, at least is true, actual and certain"- will encounter a smile an two question marks from a philosopher now-a-days. "Sir", the philosopher will perhaps give him to understand, "it is improbable that you are not mistaken; but why insist on truth?" (F. Nietzsche 23-24)[16]

Before developing opinions about good and bad and true, philosophers of today need to keep in mind that "truth" and "happiness" may not necessarily be co-related, a mistake philosophers hitherto are accustomed of making. Nietzsche asks –

"Are these coming philosophers new friends of "truth"? This is probable enough, for all philosophers so far have loved their truths. But they will certainly not be dogmatists. It must offend their pride, also their taste, if their truth is supposed to be a truth for every man- which has so far been the secret wish and hidden meaning of all dogmatic aspirations. "My judgement is my judgement"; no one else is easily entitled to it- that is what such philosophers of future may perhaps say of himself.

One must shed the bad taste of wanting to agree with many. "Good" is no longer good when one's neighbour mouths it. And how should there be a "common good"! The term contradicts itself: whatever can be common always has little value. In the end it must be as it is and always has been: great things remain for the great, abysses for the profound, nuances and shudders for the refined, and, in brief, all that is rare for the rare." (F. Nietzsche 53)[17]

Now, when Nietzsche poses such questions, as "why insist on truth?" it certainly does not mean that he doesn't cares for **truth** or **untruth**, instead, he wants us to penetrate through the very core of such ideas. That which is accepted as truth, is it worthy of all the fuss that has been created around it? Or how long will a specific notion remain to be **true**. When we contemplate in the light of ever-changing social, moral, cultural and cosmological scenarios, a **truth** from 500 years ago, is now mere an absurd idea. Doesn't truth changes with time, space and way of perception! This discourse on pragmatic aspect of truth, by Nietzsche's point of view is a whole another field of discussion which needs attention. However, here, he needs the philosophers of today to question the fundamental belief system, which we accept generations after generations, without deeply thinking about the consequences it has over the individual intellectual liberty.

"For all the value that the true, the truthful, the selfless may deserve, it would still be possible that a higher and more fundamental value for life might have to be ascribed to deception, selfishness and lust. It might even be possible that what constitutes the value of these good and revered things is precisely that they are insidiously related, tied to and involved with these wicked, seemingly opposite things- may be even one with them in essence. Maybe!

But who has the will to concern himself with such dangerous maybes? For that, one really has to wait for the advent of a new species of philosophers, such as have somehow another and converse taste ad propensity from those we have known so far- philosophers of dangerous "maybe" in every sense." (F. Nietzsche 10)[18]

Mostly philosophers work within an academic discipline by further analyzing and explaining, sometimes reinterpreting and providing a new description of the previous parent philosophical concept. But there are few who start anew. They doubt over the most fundamental ideas of their time and provide strong arguments for their doubts, causing convulsions in the conventional system of things. Nietzsche was of the later sort. With a single sentence he was able to unveil the absurdity and falseness of our belief system. He asked questions concerning dangerous **maybes**, he questioned the importance to **certain** over **uncertain**, and **truth** over **illusions**. Is it not true that **uncertain** is pregnant with enormous possibilities and **certain** are rather a full stop! Are not illusions capable of providing much more to the intellectual world, compared to the **truth?** Can there really be a sharp distinction between right and wrong, white and black, true and untrue! He paints out how we all have agreed to *"recognize UNTRUTH as a CONDITION of LIFE"*. (F. Nietzsche 12)[19] Philosophers, scholars and common men, all of us have agreed over few fictitious theories just because they satisfy our psychological urge to find purpose behind our momentary existence. We believe in them because we need to, if we want to survive our routine life, if we want to get up every morning, go to work, get a sound sleep at night, we have to believe in these theories of after-life, of some omnipotent, omnipresent power who sees all, cares all, rewards good, punishes bad, everything that happens, happen for a reason and their lies some distant good behind every misery. We have to believe them because it's easy and because not believing is far more dangerous and frightening, as Voltaire said, "If god did not exist, it would be necessary to invent him."[2]Nietzsche emphasizes on how wilfully we accept these false opinions and ideas knowing they are false but still are life furthering –

---

[2] "Si Dieu n' existait pas, il faudrait l'inventer." This famously quoted line appears in a poem Voltaire wrote as a reply to an anonymous author of book "The three Imposters", who in his book denied the existence of any sort of divine body. Voltaire found this book dangerous as he believed that notion of "existence of God" is useful for establishing social order. He wrote this poem in 1768- "Epistle to the author of book, "The three imposters"".

"The falseness of a judgement is for us not necessarily an objection to a judgement; in this respect our new language may sound strangest. The question is to what extent it is life promoting, life-preserving, species-preserving, perhaps even species cultivating. And we are fundamentally inclined to claim that the falsest judgements (which include the synthetic judgements a priori) are the most indispensable for us; that without accepting the fictions of logic, without measuring reality against the purely invented world of the unconditional and self-identical, without a constant falsification of the world by means of numbers, man could not live- that renouncing false judgements would mean renouncing life and a denial of life. " (F. Nietzsche 11-12)[20]

He further says that most philosophers are generally advocates. They work hard to defend their prejudices. Analytical philosophers like Kant, who knows distinctly and agrees that metaphysics as a science is not possible still tends to believe that suprasensible entities, such as God or immortal self exist. Although they cannot be experienced yet are supported by **natural disposition in man**. Nietzsche looks at "categorical imperative" of Kant "subtle tricks of old moralists and preachers" (F. Nietzsche 13)[21], and speaks of Spinoza's method as "hocus-pocus in mathematical form" (F. Nietzsche 13)[22].

His complaint is that these old philosophers trick us by the play of words to believe what their wisdom tells them, and most of all they pose it to be the only truth. He also finds the obvious contradiction in the ideas proposed by ancient philosophers and a lack of practical understanding of their theories. He takes stoic philosophers for example, as we know the basic rule of cynic and stoic philosophy is 'go back to nature', for stoic philosophers, universe is rational and man is a part of it. Living with nature, for them means living in harmony with nature, but then they give complete control of human actions to some kind of innate law of cosmos.

"Again a man is said to be free when knowing the laws of nature, acts according to this knowledge. In other words, man is rational when he is under control of his own reason and in accordance with the reason of the world. A man is said to be free when he acts in accordance with his rational nature or thoughtful choice and assent. A man is free only in the sense of rational self-determination." (Masih, A critical History of Western Philosophy 122)[23]

What sort of freedom is this? And how is it **living in harmony with nature,** when man is supposed to submit completely to some superficial **rational nature,** and everything that comes naturally to human beings , say, feelings, passion, emotions, are all external elements to this **rational nature**. Man is supposed to be devoid of his basic natural instincts and bound to live a life of asceticism.

"According to nature" you want to live? O you noble Stoics, what deceptive words these are! Imagine a being like nature, wasteful beyond measure, indifferent beyond measure, without purpose and consideration, without mercy and justice, fertile and desolate and uncertain at the same time; imagine indifference itself as a power – how could you live according to this indifference?... and supposing your imperative "live according to nature" meant at bottom as much as "live according to life"- how could you NOT do that? Why make a principle of what you yourself are and must be? ...

...Your pride wants to impose your morality, your ideal, on nature – even on nature – and incorporate them in her; you demand that she should be nature "according to the stoa", and you would like all existence to exist only after your own image – as an immense external glorification and generalization of Stoicism, for all your love of truth, you have forced yourselves so long, so persistently, so rigidly- hypnotically to see nature the wrong way, namely stoically, that you are no longer able to see her differently." (F. Nietzsche 15-16)[24]

But then Nietzsche says, *"What formerly happened with the stoics, still happens today too, as soon as any philosophy begins to believe in itself. It always creates a world in its own image; it cannot do otherwise."* (F. Nietzsche 16)[25]

There is a long list of misinterpreted and misunderstood concepts due to **prejudices of philosophers**; which needs to be sorted out. Like, Aristotelian tradition held that one could work out all the laws that govern the universe by pure thoughts; it was not necessary to check them by observation[26]. Further Aristotle believed that one could not give an event an absolute position in space, but both Aristotle and Newton believed in Absolute time[27]. Kant on the other hand believed time and space are first and foremost modes of perception and not attributes of the physical world, i.e. time and space does not exist on their own. He called the phenomenon perceived by time and space "appearance", because we perceive it within the limitation of our minds, and as far as reality is concerned, he said there is no way we could know it. Einstein, later on rejected the notion of Absolute Time –

"However, in a famous paper in 1905, a hitherto unknown clerk in the Swiss patent office, Albert Einstein, pointed out that the whole idea of an ether was unnecessary providing one was willing to abandon the idea of absolute time."[28] In his general theory of relativity (1915), *"Einstein made a revolutionary suggestion that Gravity is not a force like other forces, but is a consequence of the fact that space-time is not flat as has been previously assumed, it is curved or "wrapped", by the distribution of mass and energy in it... In general relativity, bodies always follow straight lines in four-dimensional space-time, but they nevertheless appear to us to move along curved paths in our three-dimensional space... Another prediction of general theory of relativity is that time should appear to run slower near a massive body like earth. This is because there is a relation between the energy of light and its frequency (that is the number of waves of light per second): the greater the energy the higher the frequency... this prediction was tested in 1962, using a pair of very accurate clocks mounted at the top and bottom of a water tower. The clock at the bottom, which was nearer the earth, was found to run slower, in exact agreement with "general theory of relativity"... Newton's laws of motion put an end to the idea of absolute position in space. The theory of relativity gets rid of absolute time.*

...Before 1915, space and time were thought of as fixed arena in which events took place, but which was not affected by what happened in it... The situation however is quite different in general theory of relativity... space and time not only affect but are also affected by everything that happens in the universe. Just as one cannot talk about events in the universe without the notions of space and time, so in general

relativity it becomes meaningless to talk about space and time outside the limits of universe." (S. W. Hawking 20-36)[29]

Therefore space and time are not any absolute entity outside the universe, but they are also not some categories in human mind through which we perceive phenomenon of the world as Kant believed. They are in fact, one of the cosmological mysteries which need further deeper knowledge and understanding.

Again, Kant's synthetic judgements a-priori is just an ideal concept in his mind which he would have very much liked to be true, but there is no proof to support his premise. All the efforts he has made to prove that synthetic judgement a-priori exists in mathematics and physics lead to more and more absurdities. In an expression 'x+y=z', 'z' will always be contained in 'x+y', no matter how much bigger or smaller values are assigned to these variables, and it clearly makes the expression analytic, not synthetic. Also, in physics, the premises, in order to be accepted as valid knowledge, need to be verified by experience, which makes them synthetic but a-posteriori. Same is the problem with Kant's categorical imperatives. An imperative is something a person must do and it is categorical if it is true at all times. This whole effort of seeking finality, something that will be true at all times and all circumstances in science is a blunder. Every scientific theory is bound to live by the risk of being proved wrong any minute. Same is with philosophy, this risk of being proved wrong, falling on its face and standing again with some new truths is the beauty of it. Kant forcing the idea of God is much more like Newton refusing to accept lack of absolute space, even though it was implied by his laws, because it did not accord with the idea of God (S. W.

Hawking 18)[30]. Kant believed there are limits to what we can know, I say, there isn't, we can know everything there is, maybe we just need more time, maybe we need develop better skills, maybe we need to be more evolved, and this is when new order of philosopher intervenes. What Nietzsche says about Kant's synthetic judgements a-priori is worth taking a look –

"*... and it's high time to replace the Kantian question, 'How are synthetic judgements a-priori possible?' by another question, 'Why is belief in such judgements necessary?'*" (F. Nietzsche 47)[31]

Philosophical thoughts all over the world tend to somehow connect to one or other typical academic history of thoughts. There are few **fundamental schemes of philosophizing**, as Nietzsche calls them, and each philosophy willingly or unwillingly falls to one of these **fundamental schemes**. This is why there can be seen a family resemblance in Indian, Greek and German philosophizing, because all of them are "*unconsciously dominated by similar grammatical functions*". There are more or less similar needs and similar thinking patterns of human mind all over the world, similar solutions to similar problems. Men, when they find no consolation in this world, they start to romanticize the situation, they choose to create an illusion, they imagine a perfect world with everything good in it where they hope to go after they go through every ups and down of this mortal universe. This fictional world gives them hope and courage to go on. That's the central idea of every mythology, every religion, and every philosophy of absolutism. That's the resemblance in Indian, Greek and German philosophizing. That's the reason behind the concepts of "Brahman satya jagannmitthya", "real and apparent worlds", "concrete universals" and so on. What's objectionable is that, philosophers in every generation study the theories before them propounded in west and in orient, and continue to either agree or disagree with them, limiting the growth of original ideas. The first thing every student of philosophy does is reading a book. He reads and contemplates what is already written and unconsciously falls into the loop of agreeing and disagreeing with the same fundamental concepts contributing nothing new. Nietzsche describes what a scholar goes through when he reads a book in **Ecce Homo** –

"Let me take as an analogy one's dealings with books. The scholar, who basically just 'skims' books- on a moderate day the classicist gets through roughly 200- ends up completely losing the ability to think for himself. If he does not skim, he does not think. He respond to a stimulus (an idea he has read) when he thinks- he ends up just reacting. The scholar expands all his strength in saying 'yes' and 'no', in critiquing what has already been thought- he himself no longer thinks... the instincts for self-defence has been worn down in him; otherwise he would defend himself against books...

...-In the early morning at break of day, when you are at your freshest, at the dawning of your strength, to read a book- that is what I call depraved!" (F. Nietzsche, Ecce Homo 31)[32]

This analogy does not only show his deep yearning for original thoughts but also reflects the depth of his understanding of how conditioned our minds are! And where we lack the effort it takes from being ordinary to extra-ordinary. Philosophy gives us the opportunity to excel everything that conditions our mind. We can start with a childlike wonder towards everything that comes to our path and look with more of a phenomenological approach (by the reduction and bracketing of what we have already read) to the philosophical questions like **who are we? Where do we come from? What comes after? What's the purpose of the universe?** And most importantly **How to cope with this absurdity!** About his own philosophy Nietzsche says in the foreword of Ecce Homo–

"I would prefer to be a satyr rather than saint. But just read this work. Perhaps I have managed to express this contrast in a cheerful and benevolent way, perhaps, that was the only point of this work. The last thing I would promise would be to 'improve' humanity. I do not set up any new idols; let the old ones learn what it means to have the legs of clay."[33]

For according to him, he is *"no bogeyman"*[34], he is *"no moral monster"*[34], in his own words, *"I am a disciple of the philosopher Dionysus".*[35]

1.2 "A Disciple of philosopher Dionysus" :

Describing the Dionysian impact on Nietzsche's philosophy is important for the present work as it explains the novelty of Nietzsche's attitude in philosophy of religion. It was the Dionysian element in Nietzsche's intellectual personality that stopped him from giving up and surrendering to the mass culture of looking up towards a **beyond**, it gave him the courage to hold his ground despite realizing the horrid realities of a godless world. Nietzsche's declaration *"I am a disciple of the philosopher Dionysus; I would prefer to be a satyr rather than a saint"* occurs in Ecce Homo's foreword, aphorism 2, but the idea of Dionysian philosophy has been grown gradually in Nietzsche's works since his very first book **The birth of tragedy (1872)**. The philosophy attributed to the figure of Dionysus has changed as the philosopher matured, but Dionysus has always occupied a special place in Nietzsche's mind, the extent of which can be understood by the fact that in his insanity he started identifying himself as Dionysus. He wrote a letter to Cosima Wagner in the beginning of January 1889-

"Aridane, I love you. Dionysus." (F. Nietzsche, Selected letters of Friedrich Nietzsche)[36]

Google describes Dionysus as the God of the grape harvest, wine-making and wine, of ritual madness, fertility, theatre and religious ecstasy in ancient Greek religion and myth. Wikipedia tells, origin of Dionysus is uncertain, *"his cults took many forms; some are described by ancient sources as Thracian, others as Greek. In some cults, he arrives from the east, as an Asiatic foreigner, in others, from Ethiopia in the South."*[37] Further, *"Dionysus is represented by the city religions as the protector of those who do not belong to conventional society and thus symbolizes everything which is chaotic, dangerous and unexpected, everything which escapes human reason and which can only be attributed to the unforeseeable action of Gods.* "[38]

But we are not concerned here with the mythological figure of Dionysus and the history associated with it. What concerns us here is the philosophical idea associated behind the phrase 'disciple of Dionysus'. In his 'The birth of tragedy' Nietzsche starts with the dichotomy between Apollo and Dionysus and calls it a Greek tragedy. Basically Apollo is considered as the God of reason, logical thinking, order, clarity and solidity, whereas Dionysus is considered as the God of chaos, ecstasy, wildness which appeals to emotions and instincts. While hinting towards the difference between two, in his work 'Nietzsche's philosophy of religion', Julian young describes,

"What Apollonianism represents is, in Heideggerian language, an 'inauthentic' attitude to death. By treating all death in an equally 'objective' way, it evades what being and time calls the 'mineness' of death, pretends that death is always someone else's problem. This means that what Schopenhauer plausibly identifies as the most important function of religion is not satisfied by the apollonian outlook. Since it pretends that my death never happens it can never provide me with a 'consolation' for it. And so, as Nietzsche records in 'The Dionysian world view', when his own death inevitably approaches, Apollonian man is without recourse: 'the pain of Homeric man related to departure from this existence, above all imminent departure'. The good death, in the sense of dying my death well, is impossible for Apollonian man.

This is, I think, the major reason Nietzsche ultimately prefers the Dionysian solution to the terrors and horrors of the existence. For, as we shall see, it does have something important to say by way of consoling us in the face of death. " (Young)[39]

Although in his later works, Nietzsche aims at the synthesis of the two for the purpose of achieving a productive form of art and culture. Rose Pfeffers clarifies this in her book 'Nietzsche: The Disciple of Dionysus',

"Thus, in The Birth of Tragedy, Apollo, the God of light, beauty and harmony is in opposition to Dionysian drunkenness and chaos. Yet, even here in this early work, written in 1871-72, Nietzsche did not glorify one principle in favour of the other, but stressed the fact that they mutually require one another. Even here claimed that only the interaction between Apollonian and Dionysian, each opposing and yet enhancing the other, can achieve the artistic ideal and the highest culture which he designated as tragic... In his later philosophy, the two deities are no longer separated and the concept of Dionysus represents a synthesis in which negation and affirmation, suffering and joy, are reconciled in terms of a Dionysian faith that includes both gods and achieves true tragic greatness. However this synthesis must never be understood as static and finalistic one, in which the contest between the opposing forces is abolished and the dialectical elements are destroyed. Dionysus remains as Nietzsche calls him, "the great ambivalent one", forever changing, forever struggling and yet forever giving structure and form." (Pfeffer)[40]

Dionysian mood is a festive mood, a chance to step out of oneself and dissolve in music and dance. The intensity of music, the intensity of life, the addiction of life is so overwhelming that it overpowers the pain and suffering. Dionysian joy consumes the being, it accepts the individual with all its aspects, both, the reflective, contemplative one and the obscure, impulsive, passionate one. Tragedy lies in negative and destructive aspects of life. Tragedy lies in the fact that no matter what he does; man is descending towards the nothingness. Tragedy lies in the fact that the creative efforts of decades in order to develop a culture can return to dust in a senseless war of national or religious egos. Tragedy lies in the fact that no matter how many theories man creates of **beyond** and **afterlife**, he can never transcend the limits of his body and he can never outrun death. But this tragedy is not nihilistic, it doesn't get lured into unhealthy optimism, instead it results into strong pessimism.

"It has often been overlooked that he (Nietzsche) makes an original and significant distinction between strong and weak pessimism. While he affirms the former as possessing positive elements, he attacks the latter as negative and uncreative... Strong pessimism represents to Nietzsche the heroic attitude of the higher individual who has the courage to stand alone and self-reliant, neither comforted by a compensating heaven nor protected by illusions." (Pfeffer 44-48)[41]

Although life is unpredictable and terrifying, it's worth living and we ought to fight for its every ounce. A strong pessimism lives on the face of death, it sees the truth as it is, as horrifying and repulsive it may be. It accepts it and keep creating and recreating with complete awareness of forthcoming destruction. A Dionysian rejoices in his creation. He feels the pain and endures it with passion for life, because pain belongs to the living, to a dead body there is no pain. A Dionysian has the skill of transforming pain and suffering into joy, the joy of being, existing, and living. All the beauty in the nature with all its momentariness, is for those who can endure its austere ways. Nietzsche says this in Ecce-Homo as follows;

"The extent to which, with this, I have found the concept of 'tragic', the ultimate knowledge of what the psychology of tragedy is, was given expression recently in Twilight of the Idols: 'saying yes to life, even in its strangest and hardest problems; the will to life rejoicing in the sacrifice of its highest types so its own inexhaustibility-this is what I called Dionysian, this is what I understood as a bridge to the psychology of the tragic poet, Not freeing oneself from terror and pity, not purging oneself of a dangerous emotion through a vehement discharge- such was Aristotle's misunderstanding of it-but, over and above terror and pity, being oneself the eternal joy of becoming, that joy which also encompasses the joy of destruction...' In this sense I have the right to see myself as the first tragic philosopher- which means the polar opposite and antipodes of a pessimistic philosopher. Before me one doesn't find this transformation of the Dionysian into a philosophical pathos: tragic wisdom is lacking". (F. Nietzsche, Ecce Homo 47)[42]

With his Dionysian philosophy Nietzsche was attempting to explore the domains of the ultimate reality, a reality without God, a reality of 'dangerous maybes'. He was on his way towards the philosophical enquiry of every facet of life, and the lure of finding something absolute was hard to resist. This passage from Rudiger Safranski's 'Nietzsche: A Philosophical biography' explains it –

"The inexhaustible is, of course, not recognized. How could it be? It is unknowable! But the inexhaustible is experienced in the moment that it becomes evident that knowledge cannot exhaust life in its tremendous abundance. However, the need to conceptualize the inexhaustible and not just give it a name is the age-old allure of metaphysics, and it was irresistible to Nietzsche. Kant had warned against this allure. In his otherwisedry-as-dust Critique of Pure Reason, he contrived a poetic image for this allure: "We have not only travelled around... but actually traversed the land of pure intellect, and defined everything in its place. However, this land is an island... surrounded by a wide stormy ocean... where many banks of fog and a great deal of ice beginning to melt pose as new lands, and by incessantly fooling the sailor who is eagerly moving about filled with false hopes in quest of discoveries, entangles him in adventures from which he will never desist and yet will never be able to complete" (Kant 3, 267).

Kant remained on the island and called the "stormy ocean" the ominous "thing in itself". Schopenhaur ventured out farther by calling the ocean the "will". For Nietzsche, absolute reality was "Dionysian". In the words of Goethe, whom he quoted, reality is "an eternal ocean, a mutable weaving, a glowing life" (1,64; BT 8). When the Dionysian is understoodin this way, it is not merely one aspect of reality but its very core. As if wanting to respond directly to Kant's metaphor of the ocean of the unknowable, Nietzsche the Dionysian wrote in his later Gay Science: "Finally our ships may once again set sail, sailing out no matter what the danger; any risk taken by the lover of knowledge are permitted once again; the ocean, our ocean, lies upon there once again, perhaps there has never been such an 'open ocean'" (3, 574; GS 343). " (Safranski 79)[43]

Therefore enticed by the lure of knowledge, Nietzsche set his sail towards the ocean of the absolute reality. He was ready to risk every metaphysical consolation while doing so. To gain some sense of the absolute reality, one has to pass through the labyrinth of religion. It is almost impossible to see through the complex web of beliefs and misbelieves, faiths and delusions. To see through the stories, myths, Gods, heaven and hell, one needs to rise above the pre-conditioned mind we discussed before, and thus raised the need for the philosophical enquiry of the **notion of religion.**

1.3 Notion of religion as a subject matter of philosophical enquiry :

The tremendousness of life and the fact that man within the limits of his body cannot grasp this tremendousness is something every reflective mind struggles with. Nietzsche too struggled with this lure of landing on something 'absolute' in his journey towards knowledge. He too, hoped to find the **meaning behind it all, the ultimate something**, something that would explain this miracle called life! But according to Nietzsche this **ultimate something** cannot exist outside of what Kant termed as 'phenomena'. In his preface for the second edition of 'The Gay Science' he says, *"Every philosophy that ranks peace above war, every ethic with a negative definition of happiness, every metaphysics and physics that knows some finale, some final state of some sort, every predominantly aesthetic or religious craving for some Apart, Beyond, Outside, Above, permits the question whether it was not sickness that inspired the philosopher."* (F. Nietzsche, The Gay Science 34)[44] It seems relevant to clear that 'absolute reality' and 'beyond' are not the same, although they give the same vibe, 'beyond' necessarily implies to somewhere outside the cosmos. Some imaginary land where everything is perfect, some sort of 'Utopian state', a heaven. Absolute or ultimate reality on the other hand is not necessarily outside of this world. 'A Dictionary of Philosophy of Religion' describes 'absolute' as follows;

"From the Latin absolutes, meaning "the perfect" or "completed" (as opposed to the relative), "The Absolute" is often used to refer to God as the ultimate, independent reality from which all life flows. Although philosophers and theologians as far back as Nicholas of Cusa have used the term in reference to God (e.g., Nicholas of Cusa argued that God is

both the Absolute Maximum and the Absolute Minimum), today the term is primarily associated with idealist philosophers of the nineteenth century such as Ferrier, Bradley, Bosanquet, and Royce. The term – in its modern idealist sense – originated in the late eighteenth century in the writings of Schelling and Hegel and was transmitted to the English through Samuel Coleridge's The Friend (1809-1810). Russian philosopher Vladimir Soloviev used the term to reality, which he conceived of as a living organism. The term has also been embraced by some Eastern philosophers, such as Sri Aurobindo, who considered "the Absolute" as an appropriate alternative to the name 'Brahman'. It is most commonly used in the field of metaphysics, value theory and natural philosophy." (Marty)[45]

To sum it up, 'absolute reality' is basically a term applied to an essence of everything understandable. It needs not to be necessarily outside of this universe. It does not essentially imply to the 'apparentness' of this world. From the big bang theory to modern day quantum physics, discovery of 'Higgs boson', studies dedicated to black holes and string theory all are human efforts to know the central vital force that works behind this vast universe. Philosophers have tried to understand the same outside the laboratories. Ancient Indian concept of 'Brahman' is explained as a powerhouse, a mystical source of energy that is imminent into the world and yet transcends it, it's everything and nothing. 'Brahman' is the unified energy which manifests itself into this and many other realities. Drawing parallels between the concept of 'Brahman' and modern 'atomic physics', physicist and writer Fritjof Capra writes;

"*The most important characteristic of the Eastern world view-one could almost say the essence of it- is the awareness of the unity and mutual interrelation of all things and events, the experience of all phenomena in the world as manifestations of the basic oneness. All things are seen as interdependent and inseparable parts of this cosmic whole; as different manifestations of the same ultimate reality. The Eastern traditions constantly refer to this ultimate, indivisible reality which manifests itself in all things, and of which all things are parts. It is called 'Brahman' in Hinduism, 'Dharmakaya' in Buddhism, 'Tao' in Taoism...*

The basic oneness of the universe is not the central characteristic of the mystical experience, but is also one of the most important revelations of modern physics. It becomes apparent at the atomic level and manifests itself more and more as one penetrates deeper into matter, down into the realm of subatomic particles... as we study the various models of subatomic physics we shall see that they express again and again, in different ways, the same insight- that the constituents of matter and the basic phenomena involving them are all interconnected, interrelated and interdependent; that they cannot be understood as isolated entities, but only as integrated parts of the whole." (Capra 141-142)[46]

But this integrated whole is not a passive static identity, as some might imagine. This interconnected connected, interdependent and integrated oneness is always in motion, subtle energies are always at work and every passing fraction of time is changing the universe along with the beings in it. We as beings in the cosmos cannot have an objective look at the world, rather, we are involved in it, and we are a constituent part of it. Things don't happen to us, we happen to things. Our every single activity, even every thought intervenes with the web of interconnected strings of the cosmos and shapes things further. We cannot know anything as certainty in this ever changing world, we only know the probability; in fact, we attract the probability of things with our thoughts and actions. This living breathing vast cosmic phenomena of which we are a proud yet very small part is a dynamic force. I cannot argue that Nietzsche had in mind these facts of quantum reality while he wrote his Zarathustra, but we have to agree that his proposition of universe being in a **chaos** and rejecting some out worldly finality seems in accord with the new findings of modern atomic physics. Being a man of literature and philosophy, he uses his metaphorical language to beautifully describe that however content we may be of our system, our organised methods of survival, all it needs is a thawing wind to remind us that the stability which we have achieved over the years is more of an illusion. It's not the real picture. All our beliefs, norms of good and evil, all these order and definitions are not our fundamental form. Fundamental truth of the cosmos, we are struggling everyday to survive, is **chaos**, change, flux. We can hold on to nothing, we need to keep modifying our ways of perceiving the universe and individuals both.

"When the water is spanned by planks, when bridges and railings leap over the river, verily, those are not believed who say, "Everything is in flux". Even the blockheads contradict them. "How now?" say the blockheads. "Everything should be in flux? After all, planks and railings are over the river. Whatever is over the river is firm; all the values of things, the bridges, the concepts, all 'good and 'evil'- all that is firm."

But when the hard winter comes, the river- animal tamer, then even the most quick-witted learn mistrust; and verily, not only the blockheads then say, "Does not everything stands still?"

"At bottom everything stands still"- that is truly a winter doctrine, a good thing for sterile times, a fine comfort for hibernators and hearth-squatters.

"At bottom everything stands still"- against this the thawing wind preaches. The thawing wind, a bull that is no plowing bull, a raging bull, a destroyer who breaks the ice with wrathful horns. Ice, however, breaks bridges!

O my brothers, is not everything in flux now? Have not railings and bridges, fallen into the water? Who could still cling to 'good' and 'evil'?

"Woe to us! Hail to us! The thawing wind blows!"- thus preach in every street, my brothers." (F. Nietzsche, Thus Spoke Zarathustra 201)[47]

This continuous chaos challenges to be less inclined towards the love of tradition, towards love of safety and security that tradition incorporates. Most religions today are mere 'traditions', as they expect one to follow without doubt. Their fundamental feature is not the urge of knowing self or the cosmos; instead their fundamental feature now is **communal collective ego** and **rigidity**. Every religion is comprised of few ideologies and beliefs, after a certain period of time these people associated with these ideologies start recognising themselves with respect to those beliefs. Their religion becomes their identity and this mass of people turns into a community totally reluctant to comprehend the perspective of other community. Thus civilization of homo-sapiens has turned out to be clusters of different traditions constantly despising each other. Humanity has turned out to be a continuous collision of ideologies.

The least one can expect from religion is to help in achieving a peaceful state of mind amidst all this chaos, but religion in its popular form doesn't bother to do that too. All it does is that, it seeks refuge in what Sartre calls 'Bad Faith'. It tries to convince you that regular attendance in churches, mosques, temples and a little bribe to Almighty in donation boxes will solve everything. It trains you with perfection in a deal where you provide them with your **fears** and they provide you **hope**, what they demand in this process as security is your 'faith'. Isn't it a little too much price to pay! Would it not be better to rather face your fears yourself!

These traditional religions thrive with the idea that their institutions are the only medium through which common man can reach 'God' (the authenticity of what they presenting you as 'God' is another significant subject of serious inspection), as if God is an entity, a product of which they have the complete copyright and any effort of knowing him without paying due taxes to these owners of 'God' will lead to hell and other sort of miseries, and whoever does so doesn't deserves to live. The task falls on philosophy to stand up and say to these men of religion, I don't understand your methods, your dress-code, your rituals and decorations. I don't know what you are trying to convey when you speak of 'hurt religious sentiments' over a book, a thought, a piece of art, a song, a movie, a scientific discovery, a building or a statue. I am unable to comprehend what you are defending when you gloat of defending religious honour by killing artists, scientists, journalists, even kids in love and thousands of innocent people. And most of all I don't understand how can you preach 'FAITH' after everything.

Richard Dawkins calls faith – *"process of non-thinking"* in his documentary 'The God Delusion'[48] based on his book of the same title. He further says *"an idea of a divine creator belittles the elegant reality of the universe. The 21st century should be an age of reason, yet, irrational militant faith is back on the march."* In his documentary he shows how a made up tale, with passage of time turns into truth and further into tradition. He gives the example of the story of Jesus' mother Mary's body being lifted up into the heaven without dying physically; how this baseless story took shape of an authentic truth over time. He points out how the story of Mary going to heaven is not particularly harmful to the society but when the same church restricts the use of condoms in an era of AIDS, faith in church becomes harmful to the society. Faith is a brain washing agent which can make people do monstrous things.

We need to understand that philosophy of religion needs not to advocate or defend religion. It's worth is not in bragging about religions instead its worth is in questioning the idea of religion, its importance and impact on human lives, human psychology, human behaviour and human history. A good philosophy of religion is the one which makes us doubt and raise objections over the purpose of religion and focus us to rethink and examine whether the whole facade of religion still capable of fulfilling the purpose it was given or not! It's crystal clear that the answer is NO, it has fallen on its face. What else might be the reason behind this religious havoc all over! It has failed and damaged humanity so hard that it's beyond recovery! The history of religions, who have **love, peace, harmony, mercy, forgiveness, non-violence** as their core values are filled with examples of hatred, violence, massacre and blood-shed

The responsibility of philosophy of religion is to see if there is a probability to improve the scenario. If not, we need to replace 'religion' with something better, something that works in the present world. It needs to be scrutinised in an unbiased manner that the time, energy and the abundant amount of emotional, psychological and financial investment we shower the 'notion of religion' with, does it even deserves that? And therefore, 'notion of religion' is an unavoidable subject matter of philosophical enquiry.

Citation and Reference :

1. Deleuze, Gilles. *Nietzsche and Philosophy.* New York: Columbia University Press, 1962.

2. Anti-semitism is hatred or discrimination against Jews as an ethnic, religious or racial group. The term got popularized in Germany in 873 as Judenhass(Jew hatred).

3. Kaufmann, Walter. *Nietzsche: philosopher, psychologist and antichrist.* 4th ed. New Jersey: Princeton University Press, 2013.

4. Ibid. p. 423

5. Nietzsche, Friedrich. *Beyond Good and Evil.* Trans. Walter Kaufmann. Vintage Books Edition. New York: Random House Inc., 1989. P. 107-108.

6. A philosophical theory by Geremy Bentham.

7. Young, Julian. *Nietzsche's Philosophy of Religion.* New York: Cambridge University Press, 2006. P. 3.

8. Kaufmann, Walter. *Nietzsche: philosopher, psychologist and antichrist.* 4th ed. New Jersey: Princeton University Press, 2013. P. 413.

9. Nietzsche, Friedrich. *Thus Spoke Zarathustra.* Trans. Walter Kaufmann. Modern Library edition. New York: Random House USA, 1995. P. 13.

10. Ibid. p. 41

11. Hollingdale, R.J. *Nietzsche: The Man and his Philosophy:* Revised edition. New York: Cambridge University Press, 1999. P. 15.

12. Nietzsche, Friedrich. *The Birth of Tragedy and The Case of Wagner.* Trans. Walter Kaufmann. New York: Random House Inc. 1967. P. 19.

13. Nietzsche, Friedrich. *Beyond Good and Evil.* Trans. Walter Kaufmann. Vintage Books Edition. New York: Random House Inc., 1989. P. 30.

14. Ibid. p .50.

15. Green, John. *The Fault in our Stars.* USA: Penguin Group, 2012.

16. Nietzsche, Friedrich. *Beyond Good and Evil.* Trans. Walter Kaufmann. Vintage Books Edition. New York: Random House Inc., 1989. P. 23-24.

17. Ibid. p. 53.

18. Ibid. p. 10.

19. Ibid. p. 12.

20. Ibid. p. 11-12.

21. Ibid. p. 13.

22. Ibid.

23. Masih, Y. *A critical history of western philosophy.* New Delhi: Motilal Banarasidass Publishers, 1994. P. 122.

24. Nietzsche, Friedrich. *Beyond Good and Evil.* Trans. Walter Kaufmann. Vintage Books Edition. New York: Random House Inc., 1989. P. 15-16.

25. Ibid. p. 16.

26. Hawking, Stephen W. *Brief History of Time.* London: Bantom Press, 1989.

27. Ibid.

28. Ibid. p. 20.

29. Ibid. p. 20-36.

30. Ibid. p. 18.

31. Nietzsche, Friedrich. *Beyond Good and Evil.* Trans. Walter Kaufmann. Vintage Books Edition. New York: Random House Inc., 1989. P. 47.

32. Nietzsche, Friedrich. *Ecce Homo.* Trans. Duncun Large. New York: Oxford University Press. 2007. P. 31.

33. Ibid. Foreword, 2.

34. Ibid.

35. Ibid.

36. Nietzsche, Friedrich. *Selected Letters of Friedrich Nietzsche.* Ed. Christopher Middleton. Indianapolis: Hackett Publishing Company, Inc., 1918.

37. https://en.wikipedia.org/wiki/Dionysus

38. Ibid.

39. Young, Julian. *Nietzsche's Philosophy of Religion.* New York: Cambridge University Press, 2006.

40. Peffers, Rose. *Nietzsche: The Disciple of Dionysus.* New Jersey: Associated University Presses, Inc., 1972.

41. Ibid. p. 44-48.

42. Nietzsche, Friedrich. *Ecce Homo.* Trans. Duncun Large. New York: Oxford University Press. 2007. P. 47.

43. Safranski, Rudiger. *Nietzsche: A Philosophical Biography.* Trans. Shelly Frisch. New York: W.W. Norton and Company, 2003. P. 79.

44. Nietzsche, Friedrich. *The Gay Science.* Trans. Walter Kaufmann. Vintage Books edition. New York: Random House Publication, 1974. P.34.

45. Marty, Charles Taliaferro and Elsa J., ed. *A Dictionary of Philosophy and Religion.* New Delhi: Bloomsbury Publishing India Pvt. Ltd., 2017.

46. Capra, Fritjof. *The Tao of Physics.* Chennai: Thomson Press(India) Ltd., 1982. P. 141-142.

47. Nietzsche, Friedrich. *Thus Spoke Zarathustra.* Trans. Walter Kaufmann. Modern Library edition. New York: Random House USA, 1995. P. 201.

48. https://youtu.be/PGOI9IDA3zk, The God Delusion by Richard Dawkins, youtube. Published on May 1, 2014

✳✳✳

Chapter 2

Concept of religion and its various aspects

Where our conscience does takes us when we try to trace back our introduction to religion? Saying "thank you God!" at dinner table? Screaming "Oh God!" while falling down? Watching our parents or grandparents practicing 'namāz' or 'pūjā', offering prayers, bowing down before a superior being? Let it be births, or deaths or festivals, everything has a religious flavour in it. Social gatherings, family unions, ecstatic moments, sighs of lonely nights, crying, complaining, demanding justice in sorrows and thanking, praying, seeking blessings in joys, everything, everywhere, every tiny part of our life is weaved with religious belief, values, morality and customs. A kid grows up becoming aware, accustomed as well as dependent on some or other form of 'God', just as he does with his parents, family members, surrounding and nature. He is never independent of this concept of religion and god.

Gradually as the kid grows and faces contradictions, if he/she is reflective enough to notice them, he starts asking questions, and in most cases immediately gets silenced there and then, "shhhh! You should not speak ill of God!", "you should not doubt", "you must believe", "you must respect", right there! That's the secret! That's the mystery ingredient! That's the essence of religions all over the world. 'Respect', 'bowing down' and 'faith' really does the magic. The elderly, the believers are certainly not wrong. Belief does have the power to heal from worst conditions; complete surrender to the one whom you trust with all your heart takes off lot of burden. In the moment of despair, it soothes one and helps one move forward, but only until one believes. But that's not all; along with a method of living it also has an element of spirituality, an indication of person's elevated self. Every religion more or less does an attempt to understand cosmos and our part in it. Every major religion has a theory of regarding origin of universe and what happens after life.

Just one word 'religion' encompasses everything from everyday human behaviour to consolation regarding life after death. So, how do we define religion in a sentence or a paragraph! When one declares, "I am not a religious person", they don't comprehend what they are denying. Those who say "I am religious" don't comprehend it either. Before reaching to a judgement about the subject, it's important to understand how deep and consuming its impact is. There are different things, out-worldly things people tend to identify with religion, like dress codes, manners, methods of praying, structure of monuments of prayer houses, deities or prophets! And men, being men, as they are, filled with their insecurities, fears and petty ego's, incapable of grasping the subtle difference between a 'symbol' and the 'idea the symbol represents', ruin completely what it stands for. As a result, we are faced with yet another tragedy caused by man's ego. A fact very subtly hinted in a romantic novel "The Bridges of Madison County" by

Robert James Waller, where the lead character, Robert Kincaid says to his beloved-

"My contention is that male hormones are the ultimate cause of trouble on this planet. It was one thing to dominate another tribe or another warrior. It's quite another to have missiles." (Waller 101) [1]

Above is a general introduction of concept of religion. When we proceed to a more philosophical understanding of the concept, problems get a little complicated. Whether religion should be considered a "social affair" or "spiritual"! It basically engages itself with both rather contradictory areas. Every philosopher and thinker reduced religion to the domain of his subjective interest. Philosophically speaking 'God' and 'Religion' are two ideas, mostly interconnected but still independent of each other. There are religions without God, and God does not necessarily depend upon religion. There are broadly two ideologies regarding God, one is 'personal God' which is attributed with qualities, and other is 'impersonal God' i.e. the God of a pantheist, that which is referred as 'Brahman' in Vedānta philosophy, or 'nothingness' in Mahayana Buddhism, an interconnected flow of energies or 'vijñāns', the notion by which modern atomic physics is baffled by, explained by Fritzop Capra in 'The Tao of Physics-

"This basic oneness of the universe is not only the central characteristic of the mystical experience, but is also one of the most important revelations of modern physics. It becomes evident at the atomic level and manifests itself more and more as one penetrates deeper into matter, down into the realm of subatomic particles. The unity of all things and events will be a recurring theme throughout our comparison of modern physics and Eastern philosophy. As we study the various models of subatomic physics we shall see that they express again and again, in different ways, the same insight- the constituents of matter and the basic phenomena involving them are all interconnected, interrelated and interdependent; that they cannot be understood as isolated entities, but only as integrated parts of whole." (Capra 141-142)[2]

These two different types of 'God', is associated with two approaches religion can be dealt with. One of them is 'Social' and another is 'spiritual'. I will discuss about this a little later, but before let's try to get a vague idea of how it all started.

2.1 The Initial men and their Gods :

There are many books available to show how and when the civilization grew, exactly in which order men around the world developed their concept of deities, Gods and religion. Till now discoveries are being made about the precise details, but we don't need to concern ourselves with the chronology or precision. We don't need exact details to understand that at some point men over various geographical regions attributed anthropomorphic properties to nature surrounding them, and developed with the passage of time mythologies to support their social life and order.

Initial men were awed by the vital force running through the veins of the universe which made everything so alive! So vibrant! So vivid! Thundering clouds followed by heavenly droplets pouring down from above, healing the soil beneath men's feet and fine scent of fresh wet soil! Lightening dazzling the sky! Huge water bodies like falls, rivers and oceans! A tiny sprout miraculously coming out of the earth! Every single miracle of nature mesmerized and overwhelmed the heart of initial men from joy, divinity, ecstasy as well as fear! Sun, moon, stars, rain and most of all ability of things growing out of nothing made initial men bow their heads down in front of every aspect of nature with love, respect and gratitude.

Anthropologists have researched the indigenous communities that have still survived through the years in various parts of world like Africa, Nile valley and Asia, and have studied their religious and communal practices which help us to understand these initial men or first people and the form of religion they practiced. These indigenous people had this faith that they can interact with nature. They believed that plants, animals, herbs and even rocks have spirits or soul. With the help of some rituals or sacrifices, if practiced properly, they thought they can interfere in natural phenomenon like rains and draughts. This belief that natural objects have soul or spirit is termed as animism. This term was coined by E.B. Tylor, although he didn't mean it in a respectful manner. The minds journal editorial describes animism under the title: "Animism- world's oldest belief system" as follows;

"Animism predates any form of organized religion and is said to contain the oldest spiritual and supernatural perspective in the world. It dates back to the Palaeolithic age, to a time when barbarian humans roamed the plains hunting and gathering, and communing with the spirit of nature."[3]

The dictionary of religion defines it the following manner;

"From the Latin anima(soul), animism is the belief that animals, plants and even non-living entities have souls or spirits. It has often been used to refer to indigenous religions, although some scholars find it a pejorative gloss. There is, however, nothing intrinsically derogatory about a world view that recognizes spirit or experiences as a widespread component in the physical world. Early 21st century philosophers have re-engaged the prospects of a pan-psychist view of reality, the view that experience or the mental is laced throughout what is typically assumed to be an inanimate world. Galen Strawson is a contemporary defender of pan-psychism." (Marty)[4]

Along with Animism, there was also the practice of attributing spirit to a specific object or animal or tree among the tribal people. This specific object/ animal/ tree were then considered sacred to the tribe and was called totem. This totem was believed to have mystical energies and was considered the symbol of the tribe or clan. This concept of totem is still in practice among various present day tribal communities, though it's not called totem anymore. Also, Indigenous people had beliefs we can relate to modern religions, like faith in incarnation or transmigration of soul. Ancient people, when they dreamt of their deceased relatives, believed that the soul of their loved ones survive in some form even after death. This led them to believe in some other world where these souls might go, and there began the concept of heaven and hell. Nietzsche too mentions this in his 'Human all too human'; he calls it the misunderstanding of dreams –

"Misunderstanding of dreams: In the ages of crude primeval culture man believed that in dreams he got to know another real world; here is the origin of all metaphysics. Without the dream one would have found no occasion for a division of the world. The separation of body and soul, too, is related to the most ancient conception of the dream; also the assumption of a quasi-body of the soul, which is the origin of all belief in the spirits and probably also of the belief in Gods. "The dead live on; for they appear to the living in dreams"; this inference went unchallenged for many thousand of years." (Kaufmann, The Portable Nietzsche 52)[5]

In his work, 'Primitive Religion' volume 2, E. B. Tylor provides an elaborated description regarding the concept;

"Here let us once more call to mind the consideration which cannot be too strongly put forward, that the doctrine of a future life as held by the lower races is the all but necessary outcome of savage Animism. The evidence that the lower races believe in figures of the dead seen in dreams and visions to be their surviving souls, not only goes far to account for the comparative universality of their belief in the continued existence of the soul after the death of the body, but it gives the key to many of their speculations on the nature of this existence, speculation rational enough from the savage point of view...

Permanent transition, new birth, or re-incarnation of human souls in other human bodies is especially considered to take place by the soul of a deceased person animating the body of an infant. It is recorded by Brebeuf that the Hurons, when little children died, would bury them by the wayside, that their souls might enter the mothers passing by and so be born again. In North-West America, among the tacullis we hear of direct transfusion of soul by the medicine man, who, putting his hand on the breast of the dying or dead, then holds them over the head of a relative and blows through them;

the next child born to this recipient of the departed soul is animated by it, and takes the rank and name of the deceased. The Nutka Indians not without ingenuity accounted for the existence of a distant tribe speaking the same language as themselves, by declaring them to be the spirits of their dead. In Greenland, where the wretched custom of abandoning and even plundering widows and orphans was tending to bring the whole race to extinction, a helpless widow would seek to persuade some father that the soul of a dead child of his has passed into the living child of hers, or vice-versa, thus gaining for herself a new relative and protector. It is mostly the ancestral or kindred soul that are thought to enter into children, and this kind of transmigration is therefore from the savage point of view a highly philosophical theory, accounting as it does so well for the general resemblance between parents and children, and even for the more special phenomena of atavism." (Tylor, Primitive Culture 2-4)[6]

This belief in transmigration of soul was the root behind all otherworldly philosophies. Also it led them to believe that there are powers beyond their reach which control their lives. They started relating every phenomena or incident around them in terms of spirits. Good things happened due to good spirits and bad things due to bad spirits. This led to the development of concepts of ghosts, deities and other mystical beings. Different mythologies across the globe are examples of man's marvellous capacity of imagination. Let it be Greek, Roman, Egypt, Norse or Indian mythologies. All of them reveal more or less same theories regarding cosmological phenomenon. It was the love and devotion mixed with a sense of fear among Initial men which gave birth to deities for the first time. Very first of those deities was the deity of fertility or goddess fertility or mother goddess, who was able to carry and produce life on earth. These deities were responsible for various aspects of cosmos, like deity of light and thunder, deity of rain, sun deity, and moon deity and so on. Further this divinity intervened in the emotional and psychological aspects of human life, which resulted in deities of love and beauty, of music and poetry, of hatred and bloodshed, of wisdom and tactics, of wine, madness, festivals and ecstasy, of hearth, home, chastity and faith. These deities were not limited to one or two civilizations. All over the planet, every civilization had more or less the same deities with different name; let it be civilization of Mesopotamia, Egypt, Greece, Rome or Indus Valley.

Men are built in a way that they seek meaning and purpose in everything, in world, in life and even in death. We have found evidence of ancient people burying their dead with food; clothes and animals because they believed those dead will need these things in their journey ahead. An obvious question arises when someone sees people they have all their lives die, "what next?", "what will happen to them now?", If everybody is just going to stay dead and nothing more, why were they born in the first place! If there is nothing more to it, then all of it is meaningless. So, men from the beginning of time are trying to assign meaning and purpose to everything, because men are built like that. They have an extra faculty of arguing, reasoning, imagining and contemplating. Men are optimists, and they create beautiful answers to the ruthless questions life presents, which enrich our culture.

Further, when polytheism began to reduce into the phenomena of monotheism or concept of universal oneness, then religion all along the world started to take its contemporary shape. The search for meaning and purpose continued its journey. Various religions came into existence. Some of them were prophetic, some were henotheistic and others non theistic. As the number of their followers grew, friction between various beliefs grew deeper, which resulted in the conflicts we deal with today.

2.2 The prophetic religions :

As mentioned in previous chapter, when polytheism started to face rejection among people, because the deities possessed human weaknesses, and were subject to destiny as common men, the faith in single supreme god emerged. This led to the origin of Prophetic Religions. Prophetic religions are those which believe in a single supreme God, who converses with people by means of prophets. Prophet speaks on God's behalf and hence is worshipped. Major prophetic religions as we know them now are Zoroastrianism, Judaism, Christianity, and Islam.

Zoroastrianism is the oldest among prophetic religions in the world. It has its roots in early Iran or Persia. It emerged as a response to polytheistic beliefs popular in ancient Egypt, Syria, Arabia, Mesopotamia, Babylonia and Media. It was a pure monotheistic religion, and refused Idol worships and sacrifices. It works according to the teachings of Prophet Zoroaster. Its central concept is the dual forces of good and evil. Ahur Mazda is the Supreme Being according to Zoroastrianism. They are against building temples and idols, though they believe fire to be sacred. It was a well-known religion during the era of Cyrus the great of Achaemenid Empire which ranged all over Eastern Europe, through Egypt, Mesopotamia, Babylonia, and Media to the Indus Valley Civilization. Babylonia was its capital. Around the same period, from ancient Semitic polytheistic beliefs of southern Canaanites emerged a race which worshipped Yahweh and were called Jews. Yahweh was the God of ancient kingdoms of Israel and Judah. According to old-testament or Hebrew bible, Jews were children of Abraham and Sarah and were the chosen people. They developed into the 12 tribes of Israel. Jewish history is filled with downfalls and struggles. They were first held captive by the Neo-Assyrian Empire and forced to relocate, and then again they were held captive in Babylonia, by Babylonian king Nebuchadnezzar. When Persian king of Zoroastrian religion seized Babylon, he freed Jews from their captivity and allowed them to return to Judah, which was then Yehud Medinates, the Persian province, whose capital was Jerusalem. This was the period when Judaism came into the influence of Zoroastrianism and accepted its strict monotheism. Initially Judaism was a tribal religion and Yahweh was basically a tribal God, more specifically God of thunder. After being influenced by Zoroastrianism Jews inherited concepts of "day of judgement" and "refute of idol worship and sacrifices". Thus Zoroastrianism and Judaism have an interconnected history. Judaism is a rather rigid religion and gives too much importance to words of Prophet Moses. It doesn't have much regard for spirituality; instead it focuses on living everyday life according to established rules.

After being free from Babylonian captivity, Jews constructed second temple in Jerusalem around c. 515 BCE which was again destructed though, by Romans, in 70 CE. This time period of second temple in Jewish history, led to the development of Christianity. It's a fairly known fact that Christianity came into existence from 1st century CE after Jesus Christ's teachings. Jesus belonged to a Jewish family, who grew to be different in ideologies from contemporary Jewish ritualistic beliefs and narrow-mindedness. He went beyond the teachings of Moses. Y. Masih in his book "A comparative study of religion gives an example to show the difference between Moses and Jesus (or Judaism and Christianity):

"…a woman was caught in the act of committing adultery. She was brought before the Master to be stoned to death, according to the law of Moses. Pharisees stood by to see what Jesus would say. Jesus said,

'Whichever one of you has committed no sin may throw the first stone at her' (St. John 8.7).

And none could do it, for they were all convinced of their own sins." (Masih, A comparative study of religions 82)[7]

Although Jesus earned many followers very soon, traditional Jews didn't approve of him. The Roman province of Judah was alarmed by his growing influence and declared him blasphemous for calling himself "son of God". A trial was held against Jesus before Sanhedrin and he was condemned by Pontius Pilate. As a result, he was crucified mercilessly. The death of Jesus resulted in enormous increase in number of his followers and they were called Christians.

Islam originated in Arabian Peninsula around 7th century AD, when Muhammad had a revelation while meditating in a cave. Muhammad originally belonged to Quraysh tribe of pre-Islamic Arab, which was further divided into clans. When Muhammad declared about his revelation, and demanded people to follow him, he was faced with strong opposition which even led to religious wars. Gradually many converted themselves from Judaism and Christianity to follow Islam. Islam too believes in strict monotheism, but unlike Christianity, it doesn't believe that Christ, or for that matter any prophet is "Son of God", as according to Islam God is neither begotten nor begets. Muhammad is the last prophet according to Islam.

This is a short introduction of prophetic religions and how they originated. If we take religious texts as reference, we can trace that all prophetic religions have basically the same origin and more or less same ideologies. Except Zoroastrianism all three prophetic religions are also known as Abrahamic religions. Noah, Abraham, Isaac, Jacob, Joseph, Moses and Issiah are recognised as prophets in Judaism, Christianity as well as Islam. Fundamental ideology or philosophical aspect of prophetic religions is belief in day of judgement, rejection of idol worship and belief in single supreme God i.e. monotheism. Initially the philosophy behind prophetic religions was the basic strife between 'good' and 'evil'. In Zoroastrianism this 'good' and 'evil' is expressed by the medium of 'angels' and 'demons'. They believed, although evil tries to shadow the goodness, human through his understanding and effort, can defeat 'evil' and choose 'good'. Serving 'good' is serving 'God'. Who lives by 'good', lives an eternal life in heaven, and who lets 'evil' triumph, is bound to live in a purgatory also known as hell in their after-life.

Further Judaism, in addition to believing God as a creator, also believed in personal relationship with God. A covenant is mentioned in Bible between God and Noah (Genesis, chapter 9, 11-17) and between God and Abraham (Genesis, chapter 17, 1-14), the gist of which is that if they work as God instructed them, God will protect them and their sons, and bless them with prosperity. The covenant between God and Abraham, which in addition to showing the nature of relationship between 'Jews' and 'LORD', also explains the important custom of circumcision among Jews, is as follows –

"And when Abraham was 90 years old and nine, the LORD appeared to Abram, and said unto him, I am the Almighty God; walk before me, and be thou perfect.

And I will make my covenant between me and thee, and will multiply thee exceedingly.

And Abram fell on his face: and God talked with him, saying,

As for me, behold, my covenant is with thee, and thou shalt be a father of many nations.

Neither shall thy name any more be called Abram, but thy name shall be Abraham; for a father of many nations have I made thee.

And I will make thee exceeding fruitful, and I will make nations of thee, and kings shall come out of thee.

And I will establish my covenant between me and thee and thy seed after thee in their generations for an everlasting covenant, to be a God unto thee, and to thy seed after thee.

And I will give unto thee, and to thy seed after thee, the land wherein thou art a stranger, all the land of Canaan, for an everlasting possession; and I will be their God.

And God said unto Abraham, Thou shalt keep my covenant therefore, thou, and thy seed after thee in generations.

This is my covenant, which ye shall keep, between me and you and thy seed after thee; Every man child among you shall be circumcised.

And ye shall circumcise the flesh of your foreskin; and it shall be a token of the covenant betwixt me and you.

And he that is eight days old shall be circumcised among you, every man child in your generations, he that is born in the house, or boughtwith money of any stranger, which is not of thy seed.

He that is born in thy house, and he that is bought with thy money, must needs be circumcised: and my covenant shall be I your flesh for an everlasting covenant.

And uncircumcised man child whose flesh of his foreskin is not circumcised, that soul shall be cut off from his people; he hath broken my covenant." (Holy Bible, Genesis:17.1-14)[8]

Thus Judaism believed in a God which communicated with them, a rather personal God; a God who referred to Jews as 'children of Israel' or 'my people' because He chose them. There are clear indications, more than once that the 'Lord if Israel' is the God of Jews and NOT the God of other races, say Egypt's. Jews were enslaved by Pharaoh, a cruel king in Egypt, from where they were freed with the help of two brothers Moses and Aaron, who were sent by God. Moses, later, was recognised as the prophet of Jews, who carried the messages of God. To Moses the Lord revealed his name and revised the covenant he made with Noah and Abraham –

"Then LORD said unto Moses, Now shalt thou see what I will do to Pharaoh: for with a strong hand shall he let them go, and with a strong hand shall he drive them out of his land.

And God spake unto Moses, and said unto him, I am the Lord:

And I appeared unto Abraham, unto Isaac, and unto Jacob, by the name of God Almighty, but by my name JEHOVAH was I not known to them.

And I also have established my covenant with them, to give them the land of Canaan, the land of their pilgrimage, wherein they were strangers.

And I have also heard the groaning of children of Israel, whom the Egyptian keep in bondage; and I have remembered my covenant.

Wherefore say unto the children of Israel, I am the Lord, and I will bring you out from under the burdens of the Egyptians, and I will rid you out of their bondage, and I will redeem you with a stretched out arm, and with great judgments." (Holy Bible)[9]

Other than the occasional covenants, Old Testament provides an elaborate account of rules to be followed to please LORD regarding almost everything. EXODUS is filled with such rules, which LORD asked Moses to tell the people. I am quoting chapter 20 for example-

"And God spake all these words, saying, I am the Lord thy God, which have brought thee out of the Land of Egypt, out of the houses of bondage.

Thou shalt have no other Gods before me.

Thou shalt not make unto thee any graven image, or any likeness of any thing that is in heaven above, or that is in the earth beneath, or that is in the water under the earth:

Thou shalt not bow down thyself to them, nor serve them: for I the LORD thy God am a jealous God, visiting the iniquity of the fathers upon the children unto the third and fourth generations of them that hate me;

And shewing mercy unto thousands of them that love me, and keep my commandments.

Thou shalt not take the name of LORD thy God in vain; for the lord will not hold him guiltless that taketh his name in vain.

Remember the Sabbath day, to keep it holy.

Six days shalt thou labour, and do all thy work:

But the seventh day is the sabbath of the LORD thy God: in it thou shalt not do any work, thou, nor thy son, nor thy daughter, thy manservant, nor thy maid-servant, nor thy cattle, nor thy stranger that is within thy gates:

For in six days the Lord made heaven and earth, the sea, and all that in them is, and rested the seventh day: wherefore the LORD blessed the Sabbath day, and hallowed it.

Honour thy father and thy mother: that thy days may be long upon the land which the LORD thy God giveth thee.

Thou shalt not kill.

Thou shalt not commit adultery.

Thou shalt not steal.

Thou shalt not bear false witness against thy neighbour.

Thou shalt not covet thy neighbour's house, thou shalt not covet thy neighbour's wife, nor his manservant, nor his maidservant, nor his ox, nor his ass, nor any thing that is thy neighbour's.

And all the people saw the thunderings, and the lightinings, and the noise of the trumpet, and the mountain smoking: and when the people saw it, they removed, and stood afar off.

And they said unto Moses, speak thou with us, and we will hear: but let not God speak with us, lest we die.

And Moses said unto the people, Fear not: for God is come to prove you, and that his fear may be before your faces, that ye sin not.

And the people stood afar off, and Moses drew near unto the thick darkness where God was.

And the LORD said unto Moses, Thus thou shalt say unto the childen of Israel, ye have seen that I have talked with you from Heaven.

Ye shall not make me gods of silver, neither shall ye make unto you gods of gold.

An altar of earth thou shalt make unto me, and shalt sacrifice thereon thy burnt offerings and thy peace offerings, thy sheep and thine oxen: in all places where I record my name I will come unto thee, and I will bless thee.

And if thou will make me an altar of stone, thou shalt not build it of hewn stone: or if thou lift up thy tool upon it, thou hast polluted it.

Neither shalt thou go up by steps unto mine altar, that thy nakedness be not discovered thereon."[10]

We can see that the supremacy and universality of "God" is rather compromised here, although unintentionally. Lord here seems to be powerful but surprisingly self-occupied. The rules demanded by Lord to be followed without questioning aren't supported by any underlying philosophy or logic for that matter. In fact, it has been mentioned again and again in books of old-testament, that, children of Israel shall not bow down before any other God, because their Lord is a jealous God. Not just jealous, but also insecure! –

"If there arise among you a prophet, or a dreamer of dreams, and giveth thee a sign or a wonder,

And the sign or the wonder come to pass, whereof he spake unto thee, saying, Let us go after other gods, which thou hast not known, and let us serve them;

Thou shalt not hearken unto the words of that prophet, or that dreamer of dreams: for the Lord your God proveth you, to know whether ye love the LORD your God with all your heart and with all your soul

Ye shall walk after the LORD your God, and fear him, and keep his commandments, and obey his voice, and ye shall serve him, and cleave unto him.

And that prophet, or that dreamer of dreams, shall be put to death; because he hath spoken to turn you away from the LORD your God, which brought you out of the land of Egypt, and redeemed you out of the house of bondage, to thrust thee out of the way which the LORD thy God commanded thee to walk in. So shalt thou put the evil away from the midst of thee." (Holy Bible, Deuteronomy: 13.1-5)[11]

The driving force behind Jewish religion was "fear". Fear from the Lord, fear with his wrath and punishment, and the punishment was extremely cruel. Even in later books of Old Testament, we find more of an arrangement between Lord and his followers, a sort of contract. Only the book of Job has a philosophical aspect to it, and that too is of self-negation before Lord. According to it, everything is done by God, even the sufferings. We must have faith in Lord no matter what happens. If there's suffering, one has to endure it, because that is God's will. No doubt this philosophy helped them to endure the tragedies of Jewish history, but Judaism is basically a religion of primal instincts of man.

Christianity on the other hand is more of a moralistic religion, based on the preaching of 'Jesus' of Nazareth. Christianity goes a step further.

Judaism worshipped the 'powerful', Christianity was the religion of weak and deprived.

"Blessed are the meek: for they shall inherit the earth." (Holy Bible, Matthew: 5.5)[12]

It worshipped Lord as loving, forgiving, and just. It's a religion of self-sacrifice. The standards of 'good' and 'moral' are too high to be followed by everyone. The purpose basically is to raise oneself to the perfection of God.

"But I say unto you, That ye resist not evil: but whosoever shall smite thee on thy right cheek, turn to him the other also.

And if any man will sue thee at the law, and take away thy coat, let him have thy cloak also.

And whosoever shall compel thee to go a mile, go with him twain.

Give to him that asketh thee, and from him that would borrow of thee turn not thou away.

Ye have heard that it hath been said, Thou shalt love thy neighbour, and hate thine enemy.

But I say unto you, love your enemies, bless them that curse you, do good to them that hate you, and pray for them that despitefully use you, and persecute you;

That ye may be the children of your father which is in heaven; for he maketh his sun to rise on the evil and on the good, and sendeth rain on the just and on the unjust." (Holy Bible, Matthew:5.39-45)[13]

Jesus brought 'God' closer to man. He focused on inner aspect of religion. It was the philosophy of universal brotherhood. Driving forces of Christianity were Love and Forgiveness. The major accusation against Christians was that they speak of "Jesus" as "Lord" himself. Y. Masih explains in Comprehensive studies of religions, how the accusation is wrong, how when Christians talk about 'Jesus' in the same sense as 'God', they mean it metaphorically;

"Christianity is a theistic religion and belief in God is its important tenet. But instead of saying that God, according to Christianity is One, creator, sustainer, Judge, Loving Father and so on, at present Christians say 'God is Jesus'. This means that Christians know nothing about God except through the life, teachings, death and the resurrection of Jesus. According to St. John, Jesus declared, 'Whoever has seen me has seen the father' (Jn. 14.9). Then, again, 'The Father and I are one' (Jn. 10.30).

St. John himself writes in his Gospel

'No one has ever seen the God. The only Son, who is the same as God, and is at the Father's side, he has made him known'. (St. John 1.18).

St. Paul also holds a similar view,

'He(Jesus) is the key that opens all the hidden treasures of God's wisdom and knowledge'.(Colossians 2.3).

St. Paul also maintains that Christ is the exact likeness of God (2 Corinthians4.4; also See Hebrew 1.3). This is also supported by the statement which Jesus himself made, according to his beloved disciple St. John,

'I am the way, the truth, and the life; no one goes to the Father except by me' (St. John 14.6)

But whatever the Christians may hold about Jesus, he never said that he was God. On the other hand, Jesus clearly declared that God was greater than he (St. Jn. 14.28), and that God alone knew about the last day of the world (Mt. 24.36; Mk. 13.32) and that God alone is the judge of men. At one time he also said that none but God alone is good and in that sense even Jesus is not the supreme good.

Hence when Christians say that God is Jesus then it is only a metaphorical or honorific expression about Jesus..." (Masih, A comparative study of religions 86)[14]

Within ten years, Christianity became extremely popular religion;

"One plausible answer might simply be that Christianity had a universal appeal in the fourth century. Rulers could rest easy that the new religion did not seek secular power (as in Christ's admonition to 'render unto Caesar the things that are Caesar's). Older religions were included and traditional centres of previous creed retained. Ancient seasonal festivals at equinox and solstices were renamed; Christmas took a little juggling with the evidence of Christ's birthday, but Easter was calculated in the Babylonian manner and named by pagan goddess. Perhaps above all the sense of community, of mutual support and eternal hope was decisive." (Welsh 80)[15]

Islam on the other hand, developed on its own, as a reformation movement of the 'people of the book', or 'the followers of the prophets'; who were diverged from the path of Lord; the path which Lord had shown them time and again by medium of prophets such as 'Abraham', 'Moses' and 'Jesus'. Mohammad, to whom Lord revealed his message, was the last prophet as per Islamic belief. History of rise of Islam cannot be better explained in such brief manner as explained by Frank welsh in 'The History of the World', which I am quoting below;

"Mecca has been for centuries a place of pilgrimage for semi-nomadic tribes coming to venerate the Ka'aba, the massive granite cube that housed the black stone placed there by prophet Abraham and his son Ishmael(Issac). When, in AD 612, one of its citizens, the respected merchant Muhammad ibn Abdullah, began to reveal divine instructions he had received from God via the Angel Jibril (Gabriel)- later recorded in the Qur'an- he challenged the cherished beliefs of his community. All compromise failed, and in 622

Muhammad, with his small band of followers, was forced to move 250 miles (400 km) or so further north along the road to the town of Yathrib, renamed Madinat ul-Nabi('city of the prophet'; Medina in English) in Muhammad's honour. That journey, the Hijrah, marks the birth of Islam. Eight years of local civil conflict followed, ending with the Meccans subdued and the Ka'aba cleared of its pagan excrescences, and by the time of Muhammad's death (traditionally set in AD 632) the new doctrines were generally accepted throughout Arabia.

Muhammad himself, a modest man, was the 'Messenger', instructed by God to recall 'People of the Book' (Dhimmi) to their rightful duties. God had previously sent great prophets, as Surah (Chapter) 2 of the Qur'an explains:

'We formerly delivered the book of the law unto Moses... and gave evident miracles to Jesus the son of Mary, and strengthened him with the holy spirit.'

Yet man has misunderstood and perverted this teaching: they must now be told to sweep away these accretions and submit to God's will. This essential first duty was expressed in the name of the new religion, Islam ('submission to the will of Allah') and its adherents, Muslims ('those who submit to God').

The aftermath of Muhammad's death transformed the western hemisphere, and its effects are still felt. Leadership of the Muslim community (Ummah) passed to a series of caliph's (successor's), the first four of whom were friends or relatives of the Prophet. Although they often quarrelled (the last three were assassinated) they were spectacularly successful in spreading the faith. By 634 Damascus was captured and Jerusalem besieged: three years later the second caliph, Umar rode into Jerusalem on a white camel, clad only in well-worn robes and guided by the Christian patriarch around the holy city.

Although Islam was spread by invading armies, it did not prevail by force alone. Its mass appeal can be explained by the straightforward guidance and sense of community it offered. All the complex theology of Christianity was swept away, and with it the hierarchy that left lay people well behind a privileged priestly class. All believers were equal before God (as they had been in the early Christian church) and holy men- and some women- were venerated. Observances were simple: the five Pillars of Islam- belief in one God, prayer, fasting, charity and pilgrimage, plus such duties as 'jihad' (the endeavour to convert unbelievers), hospitality to strangers and prohibitions on alcohol and forbidden foods- were all that was required. The Muslim Ummah dwelt in the Dar al-Islam, the 'Abode of Peace', which, within a century of Muhammad's death, extended from the Pyrenees for 6,000 miles (9,600 km) throughout North Africa, through the Middle East, and over the Hindu Kush." (Welsh 101-103)[16]

Unfortunately, soon there was dispute and violence among Muslims themselves.

"The first split in Islam did not take long to appear. After the fourth caliph, the Prophet's son-in-law and cousin Ali Ibn Abu Talid was murdered by his opponents in 661 and his son Hussein killed by fellow Muslims in the Battle of Karbala (in present-day Iraq) in 680, his supporters, the Sh'iat Ali ('the party of Ali', hence the term 'Sh'ia') began a war against traditionalist-the majority Sunni. Their often savage dispute continues today, most notably between Sh'ia Iran and Sunni Iraq, with Hussein's death commemorated every year with grieving processions, cries of 'Hussein', and flagellation" (Welsh 103-104)[17]

Along with Sh'ia-Sunni conflict, the history of humanity is filled with savage and barbaric wars and acts of violence in the name religion. Despite the core ideas of selflessness, love, mercy, forgiveness and universal brotherhood in each religion, the idea that prevailed was of 'communal ego', 'supremacy' and vengeance'! Shameful history of humans being burned alive by fellow humans, terror spread by some self-entitled religious groups, driven by this lunacy to eradicate every other faith except their own from the face of earth, seems ironic for the religions based on 'forgiveness' and 'love'.

The key reason behind this as far as I can point out, is the sentence "ours is the only way", inscribed over the psych of 'followers' from each religion. I will discuss this further later, but before, let us take a look towards the religions of the orient.

2.3 Indian religions, Confucianism and Taoism

Primary Indian religions are- **Hinduism,** also known as '**Sanātana Dharma', Buddhism, Jainism,** and **Sikhism.** Although, broadly speaking, remaining three i.e. Buddhism, Jainism and Sikhism are all included in Hinduism. **Confucius** and **Taoism** are the ancient religions of China. **Zen** is a 'way of life' in Japanese culture, developed from Indian Buddhism. I will not discuss the specific details of these religions one by one; instead, I will talk about each of them simultaneously for the purpose of this thesis, to provide a general idea.

I am certainly not claiming that oriental religions do not give importance to the outer aspect of religion such as dress codes, method of prayers, peculiar details regarding place of worship or rituals performed. They certainly do, and all oriental religions differ in these outwardly details from one- another. As a matter of fact there is very wide range of mythological figures and stories associated those figures that constitute the vibrant and rich culture in Indian as well as Chinese traditions. There are folklores, parables, festivals and methods of worship which are vital to oriental religions. These rituals and customs and methods of worships have a mystical trans-like enchantment and seduction which absorbs the individual and makes them whole. But, here in this thesis, I am excluding these outer aspects, methods of worship and mythologies and only concentrating in the philosophical insights these religions provide. Once we reach beyond these methods and rituals and understand the deep philosophy these religions carry, we will no longer need these outer aspects of religion anymore.

The term 'Hinduism' is not actually a religion, in fact it's a name given to the people who lived on the bank of the river Indus, whose Sanskrit name was "Sindhu" by Greeks. The term originally was 'Indu' which, due to alteration in pronunciation, gradually became 'Hindu'. The religion these people followed was 'Sanātana Dharm' i.e. a religion which was since forever, which has no beginning and will never come to an end. This 'Sanātana Dharm' was the religion of the people of Indus Valley Civilization, which is the oldest religion of the world. It developed on its own from polytheism to henotheism. Sanātana-dharma basically is a way of life based on the teachings of Vedas. These Vedas are said to be revealed to the ancient seers. The knowledge in Vedas has been orally transmitted for generations and not everyone is able to comprehend it. Vedas are, Ṛgveda, Sāmveda, Yajurveda, Atharvaveda. These Vedas are compilation of Sanskrit verses and hymns covering every aspect of life and knowledge, whether it is medicine, social-science, politics, environment, art, music, archaeology or cosmology. These verses called 'sutras' are in ancient Vedic Sanskrit. One requires a thorough knowledge of Vedic Sanskrit to understand these sutras.

The philosophical ideas of these Vedas were further explained in 'Upaniṣads'. These Upaniṣads are not to be solely understood by one's own self; instead one requires a teacher/ 'Guru' to truly understand what these

Upaniṣads refer to. The knowledge in these books has been called 'guhya-vidya' or sacred secret knowledge and is given to only those who are worthy of it. The philosophy in these books range from polytheism, monism, pantheism theism to even super-theism, upon interpretation these ideas give rise to multiple schools of Indian philosophy, which needs not to be discussed here. The fine amalgam of all these sects and philosophies constitutes 'Indian religion'.

"Hinduism cannot be called a philosophy, nor is it a well defined religion. It is, rather, a large and complex socio-religious organism consisting of innumerable sects, cults and philosophical systems and involving various rituals, ceremonies and spiritual disciplines, as well as the worship of countless gods and goddesses. The many facets of this complex and yet persistent and powerful spiritual tradition mirror the geographical, racial, linguistic and cultural complexities of India's vast subcontinent. The manifestations of Hinduism range from highly intellectual philosophies involving conceptions of fabulous range and depth to the naive childlike ritual practices of the masses. If the majority of Hindus are simple villagers who keep the popular religion alive in their daily worship, Hinduism has, on the other hand, brought forth a large number of outstanding spiritual teachers to transmit its profound insights." (Capra)[18]

Though there are many humanitarian issues with the daily customs and rituals associated with Hinduism which needs to be tackled, the essence working through Hinduism is of universal oneness. Idol worship and temples are given a primary importance but only until one has not attained knowledge to see through them and understand that all of these are only a path towards a higher goal. This higher goal is the 'knowledge of the self', the essential unity of one with the cosmos. As one needs stairs to climb the roof but once he reached their, he doesn't needs the stairs anymore. The prayers and rituals are only the means to get one's soul pure and pious.

There were two kind of ideologies working from the beginning in Indian philosophical tradition (philosophy and religion are overlapping concepts in Indian tradition; there is no clear distinction between them). One, of the material prosperity and well being in this life and happiness and bliss in 'after-life' i.e. paradise or heaven; the other ideology, which was opposed to the first one, was of an ascetic. An ascetic, who renounces all worldly pleasures, refuses the concepts of after-life and seeks enlightenment and final truth. The Vedāntaa philosophy has scope for both ideologies , as it, in very subtle manner divides the reality into three levels   , Prātibhāsika, Vyāvhārika and Parmārthika . Prātibhāsika is the level of dreaming state i.e. the things we imagine or false cognitions . Vyāvhārika is the level of reality we survive in and perform our worldly tasks, i.e. the practical reality. Parmārthika is the level of ultimate reality, which encompasses all. When one attains knowledge or enlightenment and grows out of 'avidyā' i.e ignorance, one realizes that the world we live in is just as false and meaningless as the dreams becomes false and meaningless when we wake up. Those who crave ultimate knowledge and are working towards shedding their ignorance, worldly pleasures, assurance of after-life, heaven, hell and even God becomes meaningless. All these concepts, even God, are a myth, a result of ignorance and are only relevant for 'vyavharik reality' or practical purposes. But, as these concepts serve practical purpose for the mass, they cannot be rejected all together. It cannot be expected of every individual to grasp the fine knowledge of ultimate, so provide the mass a 'hope', a psychological support, and prevent chaos in the society, a practical religion, a religion of common people is required. Thus, Vedānta philosophy, although being contradictory in nature incorporates both ideologies. Unfortunately it has been misunderstood due the lack of proper understanding.

Buddhism on the other hand, at least in its early days, did not support the notions of heaven and hell, worldly pleasures, idol worships and sacrifices. Buddhism and Jainism are said to be associated with ancient Śramaṇa tradition, which developed parallel to Sanātana tradition since Indus Valley Civilisation. In fact, some scholars believe Śramaṇa traditions to be older than Vedic Hinduism-

"From the widespread nature of the Śramaṇa system, it can be surmised that before the advent of Aryans, this Śramaṇa system was in vogue throughout the whole of India , and particularly in Eastern India of Kosla, Videha, Vaiśalī and Magadha it remained fairly strong , even before the rise of Buddhism and the Jainism of Lord Mahāvīra . The word 'Śramaṇa ' has been derived from the root 'Sram' which means to labour or exert. Hence, this system was characterised by a great deal of austerities on the part of its adherents. Karma, Samsara and liberation through austerities, may be said to be the main principles of Sramanism. Ajivikism and Jainism may be said to be   the chief representatives of Śramaṇa cult, though Buddhism also cannot be said to be without the influence of this cult." (Masih, The Hindu Religious Thought 245)[19]

Jainism, popular after the name of Lord Mahāvīra   ; was therefore a non-Vedic religion, developed from Śramaṇa tradition. Lord Mahāvīra was the 24th i.e. Last 'tirthankar', following a tradition of tirthankars which loosely means 'spiritual- teacher'. The first tirthankar, Rishabhnath is believed to have lived a million years ago and lived for several years according to Jainism.

"Jainism is essentially a religion of Tirthankaras. Jainism has come from the word 'Jin', which means one who has conquered his passion. It essentially means the conquest of one's own self in bondage. Again, a Tirthankara is one who has build a ford which takes one across the ocean of bondage and suffering. A Tirthankara has not only conquered himself, but has taught people, the way out of this ocean of suffering." (Masih, A comparative study of religions 235)[20]

Jain religion is a reaction against Vedic religions. It opposed the striving for heavenly pleasures, after-life, idol worship, animal sacrifice and caste distinction. Its primary belief is of non-violence and theory of Karma. Although it believes in rebirths, that is not an ideal situation according to Jainism, instead birth and death is cycle of bondage and suffering. Individual is supposed to break this cycle by the process of detachment from the worldly pleasures. Ahimsa i.e. non-violence, satya i.e. truth, asteya i.e. non-stealing, brahmacharya i.e. celibacy for those who are unmarried and fidelity for those who are married and aparigraha i.e. limiting one's possessions are the five famous teachings of Jain religion.

Buddhism and Jainism are similar in teachings of non-violence and liberating oneself from the cycle of birth and death by following the process of detachment. They both are non-Vedic religions and refute idol worship and animal-sacrifice. Both Jainism and Buddhism are atheist and promote equality among individuals irrespective of their caste or sex. But Buddhism received much wider attention, may be due to its simplicity and practicality. Teachings of Buddha were based on reason, and never forced. He says in Anguttara Nikāya-

"...not because it is a report, not because it is a tradition, not because it is said in the past...nor because it appears to be suitable, not because your preceptor is a recluse, but if you yourself understand that this is so meritious and blameless, and when accepted, is for benefit and happiness, then you may accept it." (Masih, The Hindu Religious Thought 293)[21]

Recent researchers have proved that 'Buddha' was a title given to the enlightened one and there has been 'Buddha's' in Śramaṇa Tradition prior to Gautama Buddha himself. However, there is no denying that Buddhism as we know it, is solely based on the teachings of Gautam Buddha, who renounced the material world after encountering the pain and sorrow in the world. His philosophy begins with the notion "sarvam duhkham" i.e. everything is filled with sorrow. After realizing essential pain and sorrow, Gautam searched the methods to overcome this sorrow and after years of reflection he attained enlightenment. Further he decided to help others shed their ignorance and know the 'ultimate truth'.

Buddha appealed to common people, as he only targeted the issues of this life and suffering and took an approach of 'complete silence' on metaphysical questions. Fritjof Capra explains it as follows-

"If the flavour of Hinduism is mythological and ritualistic, that of Buddhism is definitely psychological. The Buddha was not interested in satisfying human curiosity about the origin of the world, the Nature of the Divine or similar questions. He was concerned exclusively with the human situation, with the suffering and frustration of human beings. His doctrine therefore was not of metaphysics, but one of the psychotherapy. He pointed out the origin of human frustration and the way to overcome them, taking up for this purpose the traditional Indian concepts of Māyā, Karma, Nirvāna e.t.c. and giving them a fresh, dynamic and directly relevant psychological interpretation." (Capra 105) [22]

Classical Buddhism was later divided into two sects, Mahayana Buddhism and Hinayana Buddhism, based on, the interpretation of Buddha's teachings by his disciples. Mahayana Buddhism of the two, spread around the world and was adapted into different forms of religious and philosophical ideologies, never losing its original essence though. Difference between Prophetic religions and Buddhism was that Buddha didn't ever claim any authority of God or truth. Prophets associated with each prophetic religion (even Jesus) were rigid over the fact that theirs is the only path. The only way to know God/Lord/Reality is through them. Buddhism instead promotes to seek one's own path, 'Ātma deepo Bhava'. It, insists on 'stop being a follower' and be a seeker. As a matter of fact every oriental religion in its core agrees that 'theirs is NOT the only way', in fact the ultimate is so vast and all encompassing, that, there can't be any single way to know it. Few traditions refuse reason all-together and promote non-rational ways of meditation, for example, a branch of Indian Buddhism, Zen Buddhism' practised in Japan. Fritjop Capra sheds some light on it in his work 'The Tao of physics'-

"When the Chinese mind came in contact with Indian thought in the form of Buddhism, around the first century A.D., two parallel developments took place. On the one hand, the translation of the Buddhist sutras stimulated Chinese thinkers and led them to interpret the teachings of the Indian Buddha in the light of their own philosophies. Thus arose an immensely fruitful exchange of ideas which culminated, as already mentioned, in the Hua-yen (Sanskrit: Avatamsaka) school of Buddhism in China and in the Kegon school in Japan.

On the other hand the pragmatic side of Chinese mentality responded to the impact of Indian Buddhism by concentrating on its practical aspects and developing them into a special kind of spiritual discipline which has given the name Ch'an, a word usually translated as meditation. This Ch'an philosophy was eventually adopted by Japan, around A.D. 1200, and has been cultivated there, under the name of Zen, as a living tradition up to the present day." (Capra 105)[23]

While Zen Buddhism is an extension of Buddhist philosophy, China has its own thousands of years old religion which is rich in philosophy and spirituality. Chinese religions are practical. They focus on how one should behave in society so as to maintain the harmony and benefit everyone living in it. They deal with the everyday affair of man. They provide an insight regarding a better manner of leading life. Chinese tradition believes that there are two aspects to cosmos as well as human life, one intuitive, related to the higher level of consciousness and other practical, related to the way we survive in the world. They explain these aspects by means of Yin-Yang theory. According to Yin-Yang theory, universe came into existence by the interplay of two opposing forces, one of 'being' and other of 'non-being'.

"Yin is characterised as non-being, negative, passive, slow, week, destructive, earth, dark, female, mother, soft, and wet. Yang is characterised as being, positive, active, fast, strong, constructive, heaven, light, male, father, hard and bright. Yin and Yang are Balanced in a dynamic equilibrium and represent the principle of unity in duality. Their interaction is cause of all life" (Marty)[24]

This interplay of Yin and Yang has hugely influenced Chinese lives and tradition, whether it is philosophy or art. There are two Chinese philosophical schools covering both aspects of life; Confucianism and Taoism.

"Confucianism was the philosophy of social organization of common sense and practical knowledge. It provided Chinese society with a system of education and with strict conventions of social etiquette. One of its main purposes was to form an ethical basis for the traditional Chinese family system with its complete structure and its rituals of ancestor worship. Taoism on the other hand, was concerned primarily with the observation of nature and the discovery of its way, or Tao. Human happiness according to Taoists, is achieved when one follows the natural order, acting spontaneously and trusting one's intuitive knowledge.

These two trends of thought represent opposite poles in Chinese philosophy, but in China they were always seen as poles of one and the same human nature, and thus are complementary. Confucianism was generally emphasised in the education of children who had to learn the rules and conventions necessary for life in society, whereas Taoism used to be pursued by older people in order to regain and develop the original spontaneity which had been destroyed by social conventions." (Capra 114)[25]

It is important to bear in mind that Confucianism is not an organised religion and Confucius was not the founder of Confucianism. The teachings of Confucius are the same old values woven into the ancient Chinese culture. Confucius just paid attention to the wisdom of the old, revived those values and took upon him the responsibility of transferring those values to coming generations. Hence, Confucius was a teacher, a guru. He believed that the purpose of learning was self-realization. His primary focus was on social-harmony and family-values. Confucius believed that family was the foundation of society. Instead of metaphysical inquiry, he gave primary importance to human relations within and outside of family. He believed that men are virtuous and if made an effort, men could realise their humanity and become one with Heaven. Confucianism is, broadly speaking, a way of life, a social code of conduct, a political Ideology.

Taoism, on the other hand deals with Universal Harmony. The term 'Tao', also known as 'Dao', is a Chinese synonym for 'Cosmic force', a 'universal principle'; like 'Rta' in Indian tradition or 'Tathata/Suchness' in Buddhist tradition.

"The most important characteristic of the Eastern world view- one could almost say the essence of it- is the awareness of the unity and mutual interrelation of all things and events, the experience of all phenomena in the world as manifestations of a basic oneness. All things are seen as interdependent and inseparable parts of the cosmic whole; as different manifestations of the same ultimate reality. The eastern traditions constantly refer to this ultimate indivisible reality which manifests itself in all things, and of which all things are parts. It is called Brahman in Hinduism, Dharmakaya in Buddhism, 'Tao' in Taoism. Because it transcends all concepts and categories. Buddhists also call it Tathata or Suchness..." (Capra 141)[26]

However, there is a subtle difference between remaining religions and Taoism. Like other two, Taoism doesn't have any dogmas attached to it. It doesn't have a particular set of rules that one has to follow if one wants to become a 'Taoist'. It doesn't concerns itself with deities or worship. More than a religion, it is a faith, an almost 2000years old belief system. Literal meaning of 'Tao' is 'the way' or 'path'.

Those who believe in Taoism believe in living with harmony of the world, the natural order of universe. The energies of the universe are in a flow and one needs to understand that flow and go along with it. If one goes against it, it will only cause disharmony in one's life as well as society. One should embrace who he is and not fight against it. Life should be simple and spontaneous, as life is composed of 'here' and 'now' i.e. the moment in front of us. All we can do is to embrace the moment before us and simply live it instead of struggling with the past or forcing our way into unfolding the future, as future is not in our hands. We are just a tiny part of all encompassing cosmic energy. What we can do is to live life while it lasts. Hence, there is no rigidity regarding religious dogma in Taoism. A Taoist can be a theist, atheist or polytheist, Buddhist, Christian or just a Taoist. In Confucianism there are set of rules one should follow, but, Taoism has no rules, it believes in spontaneity and going with the flow. It promotes each individual to find their own 'Tao' and discover who they are. Instead of being disturbed by the changes and contradictions of nature, if one accepts them as it is, one could find harmony and peace.

There is no 'religious scripture' of Taoism. But, Lao-Tzu, an ancient natural philosopher of China, who believed in Tao, has collected the core teachings of Taoism in form of beautiful, simple, philosophical poems in his book 'Tao-Te-Ching' (The Book of the way). This book reminds people that they just remain aware and considerate about the emotions of their fellow beings and the earth itself, everyone can live peacefully, in harmony.

Indian religions along with Confucianism and Taoism, also known as religions of the orient focus on the spiritual development of individual.

These religions are much more than they appear on the surface. These are mystical in nature and allow direct cognition of the cosmos to every individual who seeks with honest devotion and does required effort to look within. In prophetic religions, individual can never be an equal of Lord, but Indian religions believe that individual is nothing other than the Lord/ Cosmos itself. Although the terminology used in different religions is different but all of them provide the same essential final truth of universal oneness.

2.4 The collapse of God :

"The world accepts and follows the traditional approach. The primary cause of disorder in ourselves is the seeking of reality promised by any other; we mechanically follow somebody who will assure us a comfortable spiritual life. It is most extraordinary thing that although most of us are opposed to political tyranny and dictatorship, we inwardly accept the authority, the tyranny, of another to twist our minds and our way of life." (Krishnamurti 8)[27]

In simplest manner possible J. Krishnamurti points out what is wrong with our perspective of religion. We have become followers, not just followers but obsessive followers. Our minds have become passive, heart handicapped and ration paralysed. We cannot see any more, we cannot feel, we just act! We have grown into this species of fragile self-worth and brainwashed consciousness. Anyone and everyone can tamper our thought process and we don't have the required awareness to resist it. The disasters in the name religion are example of how we are possessed by the idea of 'God' and the extension of our gullibility. Richard Dawkins, the renowned atheist and physicist uses the term 'childhood indoctrination' for a method through which people are developed as beings believing in religion, and even if in their heart they doubt their religion, they won't be able to accept it. Instead they are psychologically bound to argue in favour of their religion using same arguments they have heard since their childhood, though they have stopped making sense.

This 'childhood-indoctrination' gives rise to religious and racial discrimination, hatred towards people coming from different faith, discrimination against women, discrimination against people of colour and discrimination and hatred towards people towards people who don't 'obey', who raise questions against these discriminations! The worst fact is that this hatred and violence is justified in the name of faith. There are sad examples where 'Lord', 'The God' or 'Allah' not only approves of these acts of violence and inhumanity but even glorified them. For example the following message from 'Lord' in Deuteronomy, chapter 13, 1-5, that I have quoted in previous chapter and I am quoting it again-

"If there arise among you a prophet, or a dreamer of dreams, and giveth thee a sign or a wonder,

And the sign or the wonder come to pass, whereof he spake unto thee, saying, Let us go after other gods, which thou hast not known, and let us serve them;

Thou shalt not hearken unto the words of that prophet, or that dreamer of dreams: for the Lord your God proveth you, to know whether ye love the LORD your God with all your heart and with all your soul

Ye shall walk after the LORD your God, and fear him, and keep his commandments, and obey his voice, and ye shall serve him, and cleave unto him.

And that prophet, or that dreamer of dreams, shall be put to death; because he hath spoken to turn you away from the LORD your God, which brought you out of the land of Egypt, and redeemed you out of the house of bondage, to thrust thee out of the way which the LORD thy God commanded thee to walk in. So shalt thou put the evil away from the midst of thee."

Further this message was followed by elaborate instructions of how one should put to death the one who holds a different opinion or shows a new path;

"But thou shalt surely kill him; thine hand shall be first upon him to put him to death , and afterwards the hands of all the people." (Deuteronomy: 13.9)

"And thou shalt tone him with stones,that he die; because he hath sought to thrust thee away from the LORD thy God, which brought thee out of the land of Egypt, from the house of bondage." (Deuteronomy: 13.10)

"If thou shalt hear say in one of thy cities, which the LORD thy God hath given thee to dwell there, saying,

Certain men, the children of Belial, are gone out from among you, and have withdrawn the inhabitants of their city, saying, Let us go and serve other Gods, which ye have not known;

Then shalt thou enquire, and make search, and ask diligently, and, behold, if it be trut, and the thing certain, that such abomination has wrought among you;

Thou shalt surely smite the inhabitants of that city with the edge of the sword, destroying it utterly, and all that is therein, and the ccattle thereof, with the edge of the sword.

And thou shalt gather all the spoil of it into the midst of its street thereof, and shalt burn with fire the city, and all the spoil thereof every whit, for the LORD thy God: and it shall be a heap for ever; it shall not be build again." (Deuteronomy: 13.12-16)

Needs not be mentioned what psychological input it provides in the people who have bind faith in the words of this specific religious scripture! It's not a surprise then, that when Jesus came forward as a messiah and claimed to be the 'Son of God' and tried to show a new path, Jews of that time period didn't accepted him, which led to the barbaric massacre of followers of Christ and burning of cities. Nonetheless, soon enough persecuted became persecuting. When Christians came to power, they blamed Jews, illogically for everything that is wrong in the world. Jews were restricted to Ghettos i.e. a segregated area and were socially marginalised.

Later, at the time-period of Nazi Germany, earth encountered the shameful and gruesome practice named 'The holocaust', where Jews along with homosexuals and those who were believed to be racially undesirable elements, were taken prisoners in concentration camps and extermination camps, where they were killed in mass inside gas-chambers of poisonous gases. Following is a brief record of hostility towards Jews from Anne Frank's diary, in all its innocence, which doesn't represents the gruesomeness, but clearly shows the stupidity and pettiness implied by an act of racial or religious discrimination, not only against Jews but against anyone in any part of the world;

"After May 1940 the good times were few and far between: first there was the war, then the capitulation and then the arrival of the Germans, which is when the trouble started for the Jews. Our freedom was severely restricted by a series of anti-Jewish decrees: Jews were required to wear a yellow star; Jews were required to turn in their bicycles; Jews for forbidden to use trams; Jews were forbidden to ride in cars, even their own; Jews were required to do their shopping between 3.00 and 5.00 p.m.; Jews were required to frequent on Jewish owned barber shops and beauty salons; Jews were forbidden to be out on the street between 8.00 p.m. and 6.00 a.m.; Jews were forbidden to go to theatres, cinemas or any other form of entertainment; Jews were forbidden to use swimming pools, tennis courts, hockey fields or any other athletic fields; Jews were forbidden to go to rowing; Jews were forbidden to take part in any athletic activity in public; Jews were forbidden to sit in their gardens or those of their friends after 8.00 p.m.; Jews were forbidden to visit Christians in their homes; Jews were required to attend Jewish schools, etc. You couldn't do this and you couldn't do that, but life went on. Jacque always said to me, 'I don't dare do anything anymore, 'cause I'm afraid it's not allowed.'" (Frank 14-15)[28]

Same is the case with every prophetic religion. We encounter in them a dangerous concept of 'Holy war' or religious wars, which justifies violence against people of different faith, or atheists for the sake of expansion of a particular religion. Like in Islam, **Jihad** is an important pillar which has been explain by Y.Masih as follows –

"Jihad means a striving and struggle in the path of God-realization. Hence it means readiness to give even one's life for the sake of Allah and his message. Therefore, it means readiness for a religious war. Surah 5.5 enjoins upon the Muslims to declare Jihad against the Christians and the Jews. Similarly, surah 5.9 permits the Muslims to declare Jihad against all atheists who do not accept Islam. Again surah 2.190 enjoins the Muslims to declare Jihad in self-defence. All those Muslims who die in this kind of religious wars are regarded as martyrs who immediately pass into paradise (surah 2.154; 3:169, 195)." (Masih, A comparative study of religions 121)[29]

This concept of 'holy war', works as a provocative factor to the extremists. It has resulted in genocides, massacres and heart-wrenching acts in part of men. In Israel-Gaza conflict 2014, thousands of human were killed, most of whom were children. Bangladesh liberation war lead to the massive genocide in which Hindus were slaughtered, robbed of their homes and women and girls raped. The incident of 16 December 2014, in Peshawar Pakistan, where 6 men with guns entered in an army school and relentlessly killed children between ages 8 to 18. In 11 September 2001, 19 lunatics hijacked four planes in United States; two of the planes were crashed into the 'World Trade Centre' building also known as the 'twin towers. Third one was crashed into the headquarters of the U.S. department of defence also known as 'pentagon' and fourth one was crashed into a field. In March 2001, 'Buddhas of Bamiyan', the 35 and 53 meters tall statues of Gautam Buddha in Bamyan valley of Afganistan, were destroyed by Taliban with the help of dynamite. A variation of Sunni Muslim community, Rohingya Muslim, who lived in 'Rakhine', Myanmar have been facing hostility and violence, their houses being burned, women being raped and people being massacred by locals. According to them, these people do not belong there and therefore they have the right of this monstrosity. On 6 December, 1992, a crowd who claimed themselves to be 'Kar Sevaks', a term for someone who provides free service to a religious cause, took upon them to demolish the 'Babri Mosque' in Ayodhya, India. This mosque was build by Mir Bagi, a Mugal General in 16th century. As per these 'Kar Sevaks', the mosque was built at the birth place of Hindu Lord 'Rama, hence their lunacy is justified. On 7 January 2015, two men entered into the office of French weekly newspaper Charlie Hebdo in Paris and killed 12 people. These men belonged to Islamist terrorist group Al-Qaeda's branch. They were angry from the newspaper for its satirical cartoons of Muhammad. Though it should be mentioned that the newspaper was not specifically against Islam, instead it is a known newspaper famous for being extremely secularist and publishing anti-religious materials against all organised religions.

An unfortunate example of religion working as a toxic agent is the partition of India and Pakistan. After fighting together for almost 100 years against the British rule and their tortures the Hindus and Muslims in India finally freed themselves from the British in 1947 but they were defeated by their religious insecurities; which led them towards a decision of parting India into two nations based on religion. Paper works were carried out, boundaries decided; 'Pakistan' was the nation of Muslims and India though a secular nation on paper, was a place for Hindus. Countless families were uprooted from their homelands and tossed around the border. A chaos was generated and amidst that chaos the hideous faces of humanity emerged, covering their faces with masks. Mask of 'Hindu', mask of 'Muslim'; but there was no 'Hindu', there was no 'Muslim', there was no 'God', those were 'men', biggest monster of all. Men raping even the dead bodies of women, men burning men alive, men snatching jewelleries out of dying bodies, men mutilating men, men cutting open wombs of pregnant women, men smashing babies heads in front of their mothers, men flaunting the 'heads' and 'genitals' of men they cut-off with pride! Where such hatred did came from? Was religion doing this? Was religion NOT doing this? Did religion stop this!

This madness is not just limited to barbarism. There are innumerable incidents of pure stupidity due to religious superstitions and rigidity which has been causing serious harm to the society. It's impossible to mention all of them here in this small work. The weird and sometimes hazardous customs for women when they are on their periods all over the world are an example of these stupidities. One more example is the weird problem faced in India, where people of Indian villages refused to build 'toilets' in their homes because they believed that it would impure their household. How can they defecate in the same house where they cook and worship their god! Government was bound to start a **toilet building campaign** under 'clean India mission'.

Every religion has a history of ill-treatment towards women, financially or socially weak and hatred towards a faith different than their own. Sometimes this suspicion develops into insecurity and insecurity grows to an extent where they harm others, even kill. Obviously people involved in these incidents mentioned above had their reasons and justifications. They all were brainwashed by some or other ideologies. It's not a question of which religion is to be held accountable. Instead, it's high time we realize that religion is not good enough unless is adapts with the current paradigm shift of social structure and needs of the contemporary society. Hostility for an individual solely based on his community, religion, ethnicity, race or colour, doesn't claims anything about that individual, but it sure does tells a lot about the person holding the hostility and his faith! 'God' collapsed, when it became an excuse for stupidity, hypocrisy, laziness, barbarism and inhumanity.

Citations and References

1. Waller, Robert James. *The Bridges of Madison County.* U.K.: Penguin Random House, 1992. P. 101.

2. Capra, Fritjof. *The Tao of Physics.* Chennai: Thomson Press(India) Ltd., 1982. P. 141-142.

3. https://themindsjournal.com/animism/

4. Marty, Charles Taliaferro and Elsa J., ed. *A Dictionary of Philosophy and Religion.* New Delhi: Bloomsbury Publishing India Pvt. Ltd., 2017.

5. Kaufmann Walter, ed. *The portable Nietzsche.* London: Penguin Books Ltd., 1959. P. 52.

6. Tylor, Edward B. *Primitive Culture.* 4th ed. Vol. 2. London: John Murray Publishers, 1903. P. 2-4.

7. Msih, Y. *A comparative study of religions.* New Delhi: Motilal Banarasidass Publishers, 1933. P. 82.

8. Holy Bible. King James Version. New York: Random House Publication, 2001. Genesis: 17.1-14.

9. Ibid.

10. Ibid. Exodus: 20.

11. Ibid. Deuteronomy: 13.1-5.

12. Ibid. Matthew: 5.5.

13. Ibid. 5. 39-45.

14. Masih, Y. *A comparative study of religions.* New Delhi: Motilal Banarasidass Publishers, 1933. P. 86.

15. Welsh, Frank. *The History of the world.* U.K.: Hachette Books, 2013. P. 80.

16. Ibid. p. 101-103.

17. Ibid. p. 103-104.

18. Capra, Fritjof. *The Tao of Physics.* Chennai: Thomson Press (India) Ltd., 1982.

19. Masih, Y. *The Hindu Religious Though.* Delhi: Motilal Banarasidass, 1983. P. 245.

20. Masih, Y. *A comparative study of religions.* New Delhi: Motilal Banarasidass Publishers, 1933. P. 235.

21. Masih, Y. *The Hindu Religious Though.* Delhi: Motilal Banarasidass, 1983. P. 293.

22. Capra, Fritjof. *The Tao of Physics.* Chennai: Thomson Press (India) Ltd., 1982. P. 105.

23. Ibid.

24. Marty, Charles Taliaferro and Elsa J., ed. *A Dictionary of Philosophy and Religion.* New Delhi: Bloomsbury Publishing India Pvt. Ltd., 2017.

25. Capra, Fritjof. *The Tao of Physics.* Chennai: Thomson Press (India) Ltd., 1982. P. 114.

26. Ibid. p. 141.

27. Krishnamurti, J. *Freedom from the known.* England: Krishnamurti Foundation Trust, 1969. P. 8.

28. Frank, Anne. *Diary of a young Girl.* Ed. Otto H. Frank. Trans. Susan Massotty. India: Penguin Books India, 2001. P. 14-15.

29. Masih, Y. *A comparative study of religions.* New Delhi: Motilal Banarasidass Publishers, 1933. P. 121.

✱✱✱

Chapter 3

Existential approach towards Religion

When we say an 'existentialist approach', to quote Sartre, *"we mean that man first exists: he materializes in the world, encounters himself, and only afterward defines himself... Prior to that projection of the self, nothing exists, not even in divine intelligence, and man shall attain existence only when he is what he projects himself to be- not what he would like to be....If however, existence truly does precede essence, man is responsible for what he is. Thus, the first effect of existentialism is to make everyman conscious of what he is, and to make him solely responsible for his own existence."* (Sartre, Existentialism is a Humanism 22-23)[1]

Basically an existentialist approach is one which puts individual in the centre of its thinking process, while traditional religions in their 'collective communal ego' discussed before, show a complete disregard for individual consciousness, their needs and expectations, and treat them as lab-rats (in a sense that what works for one works for all), as we have seen in both prophetic and oriental religions except for Taoism. An existentialist approach might ease the situation a little bit, as it gives priority to individual preferences. There is no denying that in our daily experiences all of us do feel some set-backs or complex feelings that one cannot explain as one don't even recognise them. On occasions a person feels belittled, unimportant, ugly, not loved, but the same person on a comparatively better day feels confident, full of joy, capable of so many things. A specific individual may be weak at a specific time but extraordinarily strong at a different circumstance. One particular individual has many different aspects within him. An otherwise mediocre man can excel in painting or dancing. There are individuals with so many different individualities within them. Who is to decide, which one of them is better; which way of thinking or living is 'right', which values and morals fit for whom! One ideology can't work for everyone. Existentialism, being all about individual choices and priorities, cannot itself be defined as a proper school of thought. Everyone belonging to this philosophy have their unique perspective towards life and world. The only thing common in them is that they give priority to 'man' over 'masses'.

For example Nietzsche is despiteful towards the stupid and calls for risking people their comfort zones, choose a life of danger, emotional struggle and intellectual pain to seek the truth, gain courage to look behind the well decorated curtains of society, religions and morality. On the other hand Dostoevsky's 'man' feels restless in his consciousness. A completely opposite view from Nietzsche's can be seen in Dostoevsky's 'Notes from underground'; His 'man' of 40 shows complete disregard for the intellectual capabilities of a mankind or what he calls acute consciousness. Instead, he is frustrated by it. He rather envy's the 'stupid man', saying perhaps a normal man should be stupid. But in the end, both, Nietzsche and Dostoevsky like any other existential thinker defend a man's 'individuality';

"But I repeat for the hundredth time that there is one case and only one, when a man can consciously and purposely desire for himself what is positively harmful and stupid, even the very height of stupidity, and that is when he claims the right to desire even the height of stupidity and not be bound by the obligation of wanting only what is sensible. After all, this height of stupidity, this whim, may be for us, gentlemen, the greatest benefit on earth, especially in some cases. And in particular it may be the greatest of all benefits even when it does us the obvious harm and contradicts all our reason's soundest conclusions on the subject of what is beneficial- because it does at any rate preserve what is dear and extremely important to us, that is our personality and our individuality." (Dostoevsky 36) [2]

In the end it's all about what suits a specific individual. Those who are looking for mental peace should be allowed to have it, those who want to seek for a higher meaning, should have a chance for it, and finally those who want nothing else but just good food for the appetite, sound sleep at night and pleasures to the senses, need not to be frowned upon. But then what solution does existentialism offers? Doesn't it mean that the things remain the same as they are! Well, the difference lies in 'conscious choice'. Instead of the adherence to the traditional ideas passed on to an individual unconsciously or unwillingly, one needs to be aware of what he is adhering to. Why is he doing what he is doing? Does he really believe in those ideologies with all his heart and mind? Instead of passively surrendering to conformity, an individual must be aware of the choice he makes. That's what makes the difference. That's what an existentialist approach means.

Now, according to the popular belief, existentialism and religion are opposite concepts. It's not practical to relate those two notions, because their core ideas are contradictory to each other. Religion is something that binds people together, regardless of their individual differences. Existentialism on the other hand demands people to take hold of their individual identities. As far as this view is taken into account existentialism can be said to oppose every social institution or every affair that operates with a collaborative endeavour; it may be an army, a political party, a social activist group, a business, a government or even a home. But that would be to take it too far. That is an extreme point of view and extremism in any form never leads to anything productive. Existentialism is not a definite philosophy, with defined set of perimeters we have to follow to be called an existentialist. It is rather a perspective. It is the dissection of man's everyday life situations and how these situations make him feel. His comfort and discomfort, the thoughts that pop in his mind, the decisions he make and the circumstances that lead him to those decisions. It is a study of contradictions between what he is **supposed to feel** and what he is **actually feeling**. And on occasions it is an outburst of how he **actually feels** that has been bottled up in him because of his subconscious need to be accepted. Religion affects large part of a man's life and psychology whether he is atheist or an atheist hence, is hugely related to existential concerns. It's not opposite or contradictory to core concept of God or Religion. It only opposes when a 'Galileo' is convicted of heresy and is Jailed, a 'Spinoza' is excluded from community or when a 'Alan Turing' is charged of indecency and broken mentally and spiritually i.e. when an individual is crushed under the burden of 'what is accepted by the populace'.

There are existentialist philosophers who believe in god and there are existentialists who do not. It's not something like choosing between white and black, it's rather complicated. Like Sartre says;

"What complicates the matter is that there are two kinds of existentialists: on one hand, the Christians, among whom I would include Karl Jaspers and Gabriel Marcel, both professed Catholics; and; on the other the atheist existentialists, among whom we should place Heidegger as well as the French existentialists and myself." (Sartre, Existentialism is a Humanism 20)[3]

Let us first discuss these theist existentialists.

3.1 Theist/ Christian existentialism :

Theistic existentialism or Christian existentialism is the philosophy of thinkers who did not denied the existence of God altogether but rejected the idea that God interferes with man's everyday life. God may exist but he doesn't concerns himself with trivia. Moreover, relationship with God doesn't necessarily works as church or pope dictates. Although among these philosophers none claimed to be a 'theistic existentialist', but all of them focused on individual's struggle in the contemporary world, and tried to draw attention of the populace towards the dignity of 'man' over 'mass'. Contrary to what the name might suggest, 'theistic existentialism' does not propose any new concept of 'God' or 'religion' in accord with the popular existentialist movement. The classification is based upon the mere fact that these thinkers did believe in some or other idea of 'God' or 'transcendence' and despite facilitating 'individual' with its due importance in their philosophy, their theories were not coherent to Sartre's atheism.

Other than 'Karl Jaspers' and 'Gabriel Marcel', the professed Catholics Sartre mentions, Thomas Aquinas, Soren Kierkegaard, Fyodor Dostoevsky, Paul Tillich, Jacques Maritian and many other thinkers can be associated with this realm of 'theistic existentialism', because of their nonconformist way of thinking. Even 'Leo Tolstoy', Russian author, brings out the concept underneath this label in his writings;

"It was no small discovery that I had to make. I had to do what all those who seek to know God and His law have to do: to find out the eternal law of God from amidst the precepts that men call His law." (Tolstoy 24)[4]

Let us start with Thomas Aquinas, or Saint Thomas Aquinas, who was the Italian Catholic priest, as well as a thinker and philosopher. He was a devoted Christian and tried to prove the existence of God with all his might, but what makes him different from other Catholic priests of the time was that he was equally devoted to 'knowledge' and 'truth'. He opened himself to the knowledge outside of the 'Christian theology'. He tried to grasp the knowledge in sciences and other religions and instead of dogmatic orthodoxy gave importance to individual's capacity of 'reason'. Although 'religious laws were eternal laws for Aquinas, still, he respected 'secular laws' too. He kept an open attitude towards those who chose a secular way of living. Thomas Aquinas believed in his heart that there are basic moral laws in other religions and other societies which benefit mankind all over the world regardless of religious faith or belief and disbelief in God. According to him an atheist needs not to be despised or rejected just because of their religious priorities, as they may contribute in the development of mankind by other means of knowledge which have nothing to do with religion. He believed that every individual has the ability to 'reason', and he must have the right to choose his path. Thus, by this minor change in attitude, Thomas Aquinas led the way towards a better civilization.

Jacques Maritain, a nineteenth century French philosopher and a declared Thomist[5] goes a step further and relates 'existence' with 'being'. He doesn't consider himself an existentialist. His philosophy too is far from mainstream 'existentialism'. Still, his treatment of the subjects 'religion' and 'God' falls into the category of 'Theist Existentialism'. Maritain believes that the only proper way to know God is through 'intuitive knowledge' of individual personality. Knowledge of 'God' is an incident of 'transcendental subjectivity', hence, God can be known within individual existence. There isn't any other way to know God.

In his work, 'Existence and the Existent', Maritain says;

"It is something to know that God is a transcendent and sovereign self; but it is something else again to enter oneself and with all one's baggage- one's own existence and flesh and blood- into the vital relationship in which created subjectivity is brought face to face with this transcendent subjectivity and, trembling and loving, looks to it for salvation. This is the business of religion.

Religion is essentially that which no philosophy can be; a relation of person to person with all the risk, the mystery, the dread, the confidence, the delight, and the torment that lie in such a relationship." (Maritain 80)[6]

The concept of 'being' is primary in Maritain's philosophy. According to him man is confronted with conflicting duties and multiple rules in his practical life, where he have to choose, in this act of free choice, his deep subjective 'being' or 'existence' is reflected. These choices are mostly intuitive. Despite weighing all the pros and cons, in the most decisive moments of life a person chooses intuitively, and in those moments a person becomes one with his higher self, who he really is. These are the moments when a man truly embraces his 'existence' or 'being'.

"But this concept of existence, of 'to-exist' (esse) is not and cannot be cut off from the absolutely primary concept of being (ens, that- which

is, that- which exists, that whose act is to exist). This is so because the affirmation of existence, or the judgement, which provides the content of such a concept, is itself the 'composition' of a subject with existence, i.e., the affirmation that something exists (actually or possibly, simply or with such and such a predicate). It is the concept of being (that- which exists or is able to exist) which, in the order of ideative perception, corresponds adequately to this affirmation in the order of judgement. The concept of existence cannot be visualised completely apart, detached, isolated, separated from that of being; and it is in that concept of being that it is at first conceived. " (Maritain 33)[7]

Maritain's concept of 'existence', despite being quite opposite the popular existentialist idea of 'existing in the world' without any transcendental or otherworldly obligation attached to it, provides a space for individual dignity and 'choice'. Man is not objectified as part of mass whose sole purpose is to serve religious norms and dogmas. He is known to God in his subjectivity.

Theistic existentialists deal with the question of God's existence in more phenomenological or psychological manner, but Maritain insists towards 'intuitive' nature of being as a proof of God's ontological existence. He doesn't seems to be convinced with the 'theistic existentialism' as a self-sufficient movement to ward-off the atheistic charges against a deeper meaning of life and man's 'existence' in Maritain's sense of the term. He expresses his feeling very clearly in his "Existence and the Existent";

"I am aware that there are other forms of philosophical existentialism, and that there is, in particular a Christian existentialism

which challenges atheistic existentialism with a perspicacity all the keener and a pugnacity all the more lively for the fact theirs is a family quarrel. In the order of a genuine phenomenology (where moral and psychological analysis is really an approach to ontological problems and where the very purity of an unprejudiced investigation allows philosophy to plumb human experience and to isolate its real meaning and values) this Christian existentialism is past master, and it contributes very valuable discoveries. Nevertheless, I do not believe that it can ever develop into a metaphysic properly so called, anymore than any other philosophy which refuses to admit the intellectual intuition of being. It cannot father a metaphysics that is comprehensive, articulated, founded upon reason and capable of exercising the functions of wisdom as well as of knowledge. For the same reason I do not believe that in the evolution of philosophical thought, it will ever succeed in becoming more than a side issue, nor will it successfully resist the historic impetus which at the present time gives to atheistic existentialism (and will in future give to new systems issuing in like fashion out of the central positions of the long tradition that goes back to Descartes) an ephemeral but vast power over men's minds" (Maritain 135-136) [8]

Still, Maritain provides us with an outlook towards religion and God that does not demands of men to act and behave as a brainwashed mob, rather expects them to be a self-aware individual, which creates a huge difference of approach towards the same phenomenon.

Same yearning can be seen in the works of French philosopher, Gabriel Marcel. He too, is deeply concerned by the loss of self-awareness in human beings. His philosophy doesn't revolve around metaphysical realities; rather he talks about the 'de-humanisation' of man due to mechanical and routine life he leads. The term Gabriel Marcel repeatedly uses is "ontological exigency" i.e. an urgent necessity to understand once place in the cosmos and to be in coherence with the wholeness of the world. This 'exigency' is a result of man's depression and frustration generated from his monotonous life in which he just acts mindlessly as he is supposed to act. He becomes so trapped into the chain of events that he sees no point even in confronting his own emotions. But, these bottled up emotions give rise to anxiety and restlessness. Man is not content with his life; he needs urgently to transcend his present state of being. He searches for something more. As Sartre's philosophy utterly rejects any possibility of something 'more' other than this life, Marcel opposes Sartrean atheism.

According to Marcel man needs to understand his role and place in the world. This need of transcendence is inseparable from being a Human. Although Gabriel Marcel doesn't speaks anything regarding the dehumanisation caused by 'organised religion', it's not difficult to notice that same sort of mindless repeated action is demanded by organised religion too. Man behaves as if he is possessed by a mob mentality and has forgotten how to think differently from the mass. 'Modern mechanical culture' and 'organised religions' or any institution for that matter treats man as an object. Marcel emphasizes on treating man as a 'subject', as an individual entity who has a capacity to transcend to a higher level and realise his 'self' as a unified part of cosmos.

Karl Jaspers, trained German-Swiss psychiatrist and philosopher, also, believed human subjectivity to be the heart of individual 'transcendence'. His primary idea was of 'individual freedom'. Being married to a Jewish woman in an anti-Semitic environment he personally faced the troubles caused by 'system' or 'institutionalized religion'. When an 'individual thinking is suppressed by an institution, may it be a religious, governmental or social institution, it poses grave danger to civilization. Jaspers refuses 'personal God', though he was interested in eastern traditions. Jaspers wanted philosophy to be independent of both religion and science. To quote from the online page, 'Stanford encyclopaedia of philosophy' (URL in the footnote), about Jaspers philosophy of religion;

"At the same time, however, Jaspers cannot in any obvious way be described as a religious philosopher. In fact, he was very critical of revelation theology and of orthodox religions more generally, on a number of quite separate counts. First, he argued that the centre of religion is always formed by a falsely objectivised or absolutized claim to truth, which fails to recognise that transcendence occurs in many ways, and that transcendent truths cannot be made concrete as a set of factual statements or narratives. Religious world views are therefore examples of limited mental attitudes, which seek a hold in uniform doctrine in order to evade a confrontation with the uncertainty and instability of transcendence. In positing transcendence as a realized element f revelation, religion in fact obstructs the capacity for transcendence which all people possess; religion claims to offer transcendence, but it actually obstructs it. Second then as the foundations of dogma and doctrinal orthodoxy, revealed truth-claims eliminate the self-critical and communicative aspect of human reason, they undermine the dialogical

preconditions of transcendence and existential self-knowledge. Jaspers thus viewed orthodox religion as an obstruction to communication, which places dogmatic limits on the common human capacity for truthfulness and transcendence. Nonetheless, as a philosopher of transcendence, he was also clear that human truthfulness, or humanity more generally, cannot be conceived without a recuperation of religious interpretive approaches and without a recognition of the fact that the founding contents of philosophy are transcendent. "[9]

Karl Jaspers repeatedly talks about 'encompassing'. It's an effort of knowing the whole within particular individual being.

"We always live and think within a horizon. But the very fact that it is a horizon indicates something further which again surrounds the given horizon. From this situation arises the question about the Encompassing. The Encompassing is not a horizon within which every determinate mode of being and truth emerges for us, but rather that within which every particular horizon is enclosed as in something absolutely comprehensive which is no longer visible as a horizon at all." (Kaufmann, Existentialism from dostoevsky to Sartre 211-212)[10]

The knowledge of the world can be grasped with respect to individual's subjective ability to comprehend it as it appears to him. It never can be known as something objective; rather it is known as it presents itself within the existence of a being. Jaspers gives two perspectives of 'encompassing';

"The encompassing appears and disappears for us in two opposed perspectives: either as being itself, in and through which we are- or else

as the encompassing in which we ourselves are, and in which every mode of Being appears to us. The latter would be as the medium or condition under which all Beings appear as Beings for us. In neither case is the encompassing the sum of some provisional kinds of being, a part of whose contents we know, but rather it is the whole as the most extreme, self-supporting ground of Being, Whether it is Being in itself, or Being as it is for us. " (Kaufmann, Existentialism from dostoevsky to Sartre 212)[11]

Thus in Jaspers philosophy we find a perfect blend of 'empirical existence' and 'transcendental urge'. Theistic existentialism is more obvious than before in Jaspers 'existenzphilosophie'. Although, he uses the term 'existenzphilosophie', he is very cautious of it;

"One reason for his opposition to the label "existentialism" is that it suggests a school of thought, a doctrine among others, a particular position. Even of the term existenzphilosophie he once said after using it: "The name is misleading insofar as it seems to restrict. Philosophy can never wish to be less than primordial, eternal philosophy itself." Existenzephilosophie is meant to be a protest against the betrayal of this primordial and eternal philosophy by the professors who teach philosophy at our modern universities." (Kaufmann, Existentialism from dostoevsky to Sartre 22)[12]

Popular 'Theist Existentialism' or 'Christian Existentialism' comprises mostly of the theories of Gabriel Marcel and Karl Jaspers. But the most notable and earliest name that falls in the category of Theist existentialists is of Soren Kierkegaard, early 19th century Danish philosopher and thinker. Kierkegaard was opposed to Hegel's abstract philosophy. He was basically opposed to everything and anything that doesn't bears in mind 'the individual'. According to him a person's life is shaped from his 'choices'. He has to make a choice at every step of his life. In these choices he has no outside help whatsoever. Walter Kaufmann in his introduction in 'Existentialism from Dostoevsky to Sartre, says;

"Kierkegaard, however, was an anti-Plato no less than an anti-Hegel and an anti-Thomas no less than an anti-Copernicus. He sweeps away the whole conception of a cosmos as a mere distraction. "And it came to pass after these things that God did tempt Abraham, and said unto him, Abraham: and he said, here I am. And he said, Take now thy son, thine only one, Issac, whom thou lovest." This is for Kierkegaard man's situation, 'la condition humaine', man's fate. The world has no part in it; it is no help. Here is man, and "one thing is needful": a decision." (Kaufmann, Existentialism from Dostoevsky to Sartre 16-17)[13]

Kierkegaard is claimed by many to be the first existentialist. His thoughts never for once deviated from 'individual' who was forgotten in the mainstream philosophy, which was in the rush to make everything 'abstract' and 'holistic'. Nietzsche too in his own manner was into this blunt rejection of 'abstract', and he too is said to be an 'existentialist' by some, but as I have discussed earlier, he didn't belonged to any school of thought! There are noteworthy parallels between Kierkegaard and Nietzsche, though being very different from each other on the basic question of 'existence of God'. I will discuss these parallels and differences later in this work.

For now, it is enough to mention that Kierkegaard focused on the personal relation of man and God without the interference of church. And regarding the traditional theology and religious social structure;

"Kierkegaard attacks the proud tradition of theology, ethics and metaphysics as a kind of whistling in the dark, as self-deception, as an un relenting effort to conceal crucial decisions that we have made and must make behind a web of wholly secondary, and at times invalid demonstrations." (Kaufmann, Existentialism from dostoevsky to Sartre 17)[14]

Hence, the repression of individual's capacity of thinking and choices related to religious, social, sexual and other personal priorities were at the target of each theistic existential thinker, whether they accepted the 'tag' or not. It's not that collective-thinking or shared religious experiences are to be completely rejected. Those have their own merit. But when someone among that group of people refuses to belong and does anything uncustomary, the said individual is treated as a heretic and is punished for his individuality, because of religion, the religion becomes 'oppressive'. Religious institutions become a source of dictatorship. Self-proclaimed caretakers of religion take the authority of God and God is reduced to an 'object' on which the 'primitive tribal ego's' of men is imposed. Such religions and 'God' are in no way capable of helping an individual find his 'self', in fact they put 'individual' at the risk of losing his 'self' to the mass.

Paul Tillich brings a new vision forward. He tries to find a way in which religious faith doesn't becomes a barrier in intellectual freedom. Being a religious person himself, he understands when religious faith can be harmful to 'freedom of thinking' or 'free thought'. We interact with God through religious symbols but we have gradually been occupied by the symbols rather than the meaning they possess. Paul Tillich talks about religious symbols. He starts with differentiating between 'signs' and 'symbols';

"Decisive is the fact that signs do not participate in the reality of that to which they point, while symbols do. Therefore, signs can be replaced for reasons of expediency or convenience, while symbols cannot." (Tillich 48)[15]

Further he explains characteristics of symbol, among which most noteworthy is;

"It participates in that to which it points: the flag participates in the power and dignity of the nation which it symbolizes. An attack on the flag is felt as an attack on the majesty of group in which it is acknowledged. Such an attack is considered blasphemy." (Tillich 48)[16]

Having said this, Tillich explains the term 'God' in a new manner. He, being a modern theologian, proposes that whatever we consider as subject of 'ultimate concern' for us is 'God'. 'God' is the symbolisation of anything in its ultimate, infinite and perfect form. In his own words:

"God is the basic symbol of faith, but not the only one. All the qualities we attribute to him, power, love, justice, are taken from finite experiences and applied symbolically to that which is beyond finitude and infinity. If faith call God "almighty", it uses the human experience of power in order to symbolize the content of its infinite concern but it does not describe a highest being who can do as he pleases. So it is with all the

other qualities and with all the actions, past, present and future, which men attribute to God. They are symbols taken from our daily experience, and not information about what God did once upon a time or will do sometime in the future. Faith is not the belief in such stories, but it is the acceptance of symbols that express our ultimate concern in terms of divine actions. " (Tillich 55)[17]

When considered in this way, it doesn't remain a valid question whether 'God', exists or not. In fact every quarrel regarding 'God' and religious difference becomes nonsensical. A society that becomes rigid about religious dogmas and closes itself to new ideas of the changing world stops its development. The civilization which is unable to find a balance between religion and science, tradition and creativity, 'object' and 'subject', fails in treating its individual with dignity. It harms not only itself but also to rest of the world.

3.2 Kierkegaard and Nietzsche :

Both Kierkegaard and Nietzsche were rebellious in their writing and denied the systematic philosophy of their predecessors. They scrutinised life as it was given to them instead of superimposing the idea of life forced on man by religion and society since his birth. They both noticed the contradiction at the very basic level of a person's conscious, the contradiction between 'who he is' and 'who he pretends to be'. What he 'feels' and what he convinces himself that he is feeling. Both believed that Man has limited his own potentials. When it comes to religion, Kierkegaard and Nietzsche, both were disappointed in the current structure of it. The deception it involved from others and from 'self', was precarious. It was reduced to mere set of norms and social etiquettes. State and politics started to play major part in 'religious truths'. The primary task supposed by a true Christian was to 'obey'. There were few set of rules, ideologies, belief's and/or practice which were passed over generations and were established themselves as final truths. Both Kierkegaard and Nietzsche refused to accept them, but the difference lies in the fact that Kierkegaard decided to find the real meaning behind religious scriptures and a true connection with God, while Nietzsche renounced religion altogether. He wanted to take a fresh start.

Kierkegaard felt that the religious texts and institutions are turned into mere traditional obligation or even compulsion. He was not against Christianity, but his idea of a 'Christian' was different from the popular idea at his time. Kierkegaard emphasized on the daily life experiences of human and God's role in it. He found no place for rational philosophies or abstract theories in religion. Neither is 'objective certainty' has remotely anything to do with religious experience. It's something that can only be understood with a 'subjective attitude'. Kierkegaard's subjective treatment of the issues of 'God' and 'religion' are however different and fresh. He doesn't concerns himself with the question of 'does God exists' or 'god' and 'Christianity' as we know them are 'true' or not. Instead, in his subjective analysis of the matter, he emphasises on 'the relationship of individual' with God, because according to Kierkegaard that's all that matters. If said individual's relationship is 'true' with God or his religion, then the act of 'faith in God' or any other religious act is true on his part regardless of God's objective state. Kierkegaard explains the idea as follows –

"When the question of truth is raised in an objective manner, reflection is directed objectively to the truth, as an object to which the knower is related. Reflection is not focused upon the relationship, however, but upon the question of whether it is the truth to which the knower is related. If only the object to which he is related is the truth, the subject is accounted to be in the truth. When the question of the truth is raised subjectively, reflection is directed subjectively to the nature of individual's relationship; if only the mode of this relationship is in the truth, the individual is in the truth even if he should happen to be thus related to what is not true. Let us take as an example the example the knowledge of God. Objectively, reflection is directed to the problem of whether this object is the true God; subjectively, reflection is directed to the question whether the individual is related to something in such a manner that his relationship is in truth a God-relationship." (Kaufmann, Existentialism from Dostoevsky to Sartre 114-115)[18]

For Nietzsche however, religion in all its piousness, falsification of 'truth'; it's in fact an artist's escape from reality, a flee into pure perfect forms, imagination at its best, a superficiality –

"Anyone who has looked deeply into the world may guess how much wisdom lies in the superficiality of men. The instinct that preserves them teaches them to be flighty, light, and false. Here and there one encounters an impassioned and exaggerated worship of "pure forms", among both philosophers and artists: let nobody doubt that whoever stands that much in need of the cult of the surfaces must at sometime have reached beneath them with disastrous results.

Perhaps there even exists an order of rank among these burnt children, these born artists who can find the enjoyment of life only in the intention of falsifying its image (as it were, in a longwinded revenge on life): the degrees to which life has been spoiled for them might be inferred from the degree to which they wish to see its image falsified, thinned down, transcendentalized, defied- the hominess religiosi might be included among artists, as their highest rank.

It is the profound, suspicious fear of an incurable pessimism that forces whole millennia to bury their teeth in and cling to a religious interpretation of existence: the fear of that instinct which senses that one might get a hold of the truth too soon, before man has become strong enough, hard enough, artist enough.

Piety, the "life in God", seen in this way, would appear as the subtlest and final offspring of the fear of truth, as an artist's worship and intoxication before the most consistent of all falsifications, as the will to the inversion of truth, to untruth at any price. It may be that until now there has been no more potent means for beautifying man himself than piety: it can turn man into so much art, surface, play of colors, graciousness that his sight no longer makes one suffer." (F. Nietzsche 71)[19]

At first glance, it might appear as a total rejection, but when seen with a keen eye, this too is a revolt against 'superficiality' of abstract ideas, which overlooks the dark side of human lives and forces the one-track idea of 'good', 'pious', 'pure' and 'perfection'. Not everything is 'good' and 'white'. Human nature comes with a variety of shades. Individual can't be separated with his natural human instincts. Hence, the religion which refuses to acknowledge the natural human needs and emotions, works in fact on either ignorance or denial, hence is not based on 'truth' and is of no use for individual. Nietzsche reaches man's psychology. His deductions are based upon how a man's (or woman's too) mind works in their most primitive state. That's where his brilliance lies. There is no denying that his observation and its analysis regarding religious superficiality and its deceptive nature are to the point. But when it comes to the nature of man's relationship to a higher self or individual's capacity of outgrowing himself discussed earlier by 'theist existentialists', Nietzsche's objections doesn't remain as sharp as they are against traditional Christianity. He himself in various places seems to clarify that being "anti-Christ" and being "anti-religion" are two different things. By saying that, I am certainly not claiming that Nietzsche was in any way a man of 'religion', but there are forms of religion he respected.

All the religions were a result of human's curiosity about life beyond death, their desires to supersede their bodily limits. Answers of questions that initial philosophers tried to achieve, like who are we? Where the universe did came from? What is our role in it? Leads to countless theories regarding spirits, souls, Gods and deities; Indian 'Vedāntaic traditions', Plato's 'idealism', Kant's 'agnosticism' and Hegel's 'concrete universals' are all among these theories. When Nietzsche shows his disregard towards these theories, his objection is not to the idea of some form of cosmological energy which might or might not be the reason behind everything and every nothing; his objection is solely towards the dumb mob mentality, and the tendency of following without understanding. What he hates is anti-intellectualism and pedantic nonsense without providing any proof supporting it.

He loathes this prohibition on doubt and experiments. He loathes the practise of making things 'holy' in order to make them out of reach for an individual. The complete disregard of individual identity over herd is unacceptable to him. But all of this does not necessarily results in a chaotic and vulgar world, completely void of the possibility of spiritual elevation. Nietzsche is not denying religion all together. If we perceive carefully we will realize that he is only denying the form of religion he has known and grown up with. He has been harbouring a certain definition of religion throughout his growing years and believed it to be a synonym of religion. He never is anti-religion. He is anti-Christianity, anti-self-denial and anti-world-denial. He is anti to all kinds of longing for death and nothingness. But he is not 'anti' to the life-force, energy, possibility of growth, power, and betterment of life both physically and spiritually. He is seeking the solution for all this decadence, degradation of human life, this suffering and war. His reaction, his dissatisfaction of present religious and moral condition, his anger is generated by the hypocrisy of it all. And when he learns about Buddhism he open heartedly accepts it and appreciates it –

"In my condemnation of Christianity I surely hope I do no injustice to a related religion with an even larger number of believers: I allude to Buddhism. Both are to be reckoned among nihilistic religions- they are both decadence religions- but they are separated from each other in a very remarkable way. For the fact that he is able to compare them at all the critic of Christianity is indebted to the scholars of India. – Buddhism is a hundred times more realistic as Christianity – it is part of its living heritage that it is able to face problems objectively and coolly; it is the product of centuries of philosophical speculation. The concept, "god", was already disposed of before it appeared. Buddhism is the only genuinely positive religion to be encountered in history, and this applies even to its epistemology (which is a strict phenomenalism). It does not speak of a "struggle with sin", but, yielding to reality, of the "struggle with suffering". Sharply differentiating itself from Christianity, it puts the self- deception that lies in moral concepts behind it; it is, in my phrase, beyond good and evil." (F. Nietzsche, The Antichrist 12)[20]

Contrary to Nietzsche, Kierkegaard did believe that there was still hope for 'Christianity' itself; because from his point of view, a 'true

Christian' was not who lived up to the expectation of churches or Christian societies, rather, someone who is true in his heart towards God. In aristocratic societies, there is an age old common practice, that the conduct 'carried by' or 'approved by' the superior class is followed by 'all', and soon enough it becomes a socially accepted activity, performed by the 'majority', the 'crowd', and hence becomes the 'truth'. Those who act in a different manner are treated to be "odd", "non-social" and even "non-religious". Hence the truth is twisted to be "that which is followed by many". Same has been the case with religious truths. Kierkegaard in his philosophy tries to show how man loses his identity when seeks refuge in crowd, just as Nietzsche does, but unlike Nietzsche he finds the solution within religious scriptures –

"And to honour every man, absolutely every man, is truth, and this is what it is to fear God and love one's "neighbour". But from an ethico-religious point of view, to recognise the "crowd" as the court of the last resort is to deny God, and it cannot exactly mean to love the "neighbour". And the "neighbour" is the absolutely true expression for human equality. In case every one were in truth to love his neighbour as himself, complete human equality would be attained. Every one who loves his neighbour in truth, expresses unconditionally human equality. Every one who, like me, admits that his effort is week and imperfect, yet is aware that the task is to love one's neighbour, is also aware of what human equality is. But never have I read in a Holy Scripture the commandment, Thou shalt love the crowd – and still less, Thou shalt recognize, ethico-religiously, in the crowd the supreme authority in the

matters of "truth". But the thing is simple enough: this thing of loving one's neighbour is self-denial; that of loving the crowd, or of pretending to love it, of making it the authority in matters of truth, is the way to material power, the way to temporal and earthly advantages of all sorts – at the same time it is the untruth, for a crowd, for a crowd is the untruth." (Kaufmann, Existentialism from Dostoevsky to Sartre 99)[21]

For him religion itself is not the problem, rather the interpretations ad manipulations of religion by man is. In fact, Kierkegaard in some places appears to be answering Nietzsche's questions regarding 'God' and religion in the same sarcastic tone. Like Nietzsche targets the prohibition on 'doubt' in religions, while Kierkegaard on the other hand says –

"The misfortune of our age – in the political as well as in the religious sphere, ad in all things – is disobedience, unwillingness to obey. And one deceives oneself and others by wishing to make us imagine that it is doubt. No it is not doubt of religious truth but insubordination: it s not doubt of religious truth but insubordination against religious authority which is the fault in our misfortune and the cause of it." (Kaufmann, Existentialism from dostoevsky to Sartre 105-106) [22]

Well, the problem is just. Who is to be believed as the authority over God? Kierkegaard's answer is, 'the individual himself'. Every individual, within his subjectivity can know God, and connect with him. The knowledge of God is not an objective certainty. One doesn't knows God as one knows a king –

"A king is sensibly present in such a way that one can sensibly convince oneself of it, and, if it should be necessary, the king can quite sensibly convince one that he exists. But God does not exist in such a sense. Doubt has taken advantage of this to put God on the same plane as all those who have no authority, geniuses, poets, thinkers, whose utterances are appraised precisely by aesthetic and philosophical criteria;" (Kaufmann, Existentialism from Dostoevsky to Sartre 107)[23]

But then how do we know there is a God? To this, Kierkegaard says, it's all about a 'leap of faith'. He agreed that 'faith' does indicate towards 'lack of evidence'. But when it comes to God, we can't ask for evidence or apply logic and reason, we need to take a completely irrational blind leap of faith. There certainly is a risk in 'faith' but to Kierkegaard, it's worth taking. About this leap of faith Albert Camus writes in his Notebook –

"Kierkegaard is not mystical. He criticizes mysticism because it stands apart from the world – because it does not belong to the general. If there is a leap in Kierkegaard, it is therefore an intellectual leap. It is the pure leap; on the ethical plane. But the religious plane transfigures everything." (Camus, Notebooks (1942-1951) 40)[24]

Nietzsche however, despite knowing profoundly, the dangers of a Godless world, was unable to take that 'leap' –

"From the start, the Christian faith is a sacrifice: a sacrifice of all freedom, all pride, all self-confidence of the spirit; at the same time, enslavement and self-mockery, self-mutilation. There is cruelty and

religious Phoenicianism in this faith which is expected of an over-ripe, multiple, and much-spoiled conscience: it presupposes that the subjection of the spirit hurts indescribably; that the whole past and the habits of such a spirit resist the absurdissimum which "faith" represents to it." (F. Nietzsche 60)[25]

Therefore, the differences between the philosophies of Kierkegaard and Nietzsche represent the possible scopes religion has; if one is able to take a 'leap of faith' despite being unable to find any valid reason to believe in a 'God', then he gains a life of mental comfort, and passes through the journey called life with a sense of support and relief. If he is unable to have a blind faith, one goes through life, with a sense of uncertainty, despair and absurdity.

What is the 'objective truth' doesn't really make any difference in the course of events one faces throughout his pragmatic life.

3.3 Sartre and Camus

There is a wide range of existentialist philosophers, all of them discuss the feeling of 'absurdity', discomfort in the way things are and man's situation in the world. Few of them provide solutions and rest declare that there is no solution at all. The choice man makes shapes his attitude towards religion. A nihilist attitude is bound to lead an individual towards hopelessness, which combined to men's fundamental instinct to survival will eventually force him towards one or other kind of 'religion'. Sartre was amongst those who don't see any solution at all, rather than making choices between the presented possibilities and living with those choices for the rest of one's life. Camus on the other hand was not ready to give up. Instead of succumbing up to the Idea that life does not have any meaning at all, he proposes that if life doesn't have any intrinsic meaning of its own, we can give it any meaning at all. We can make out of life whatever we want it to be. It's full of possibilities and opportunities. Hence, Sartre and Camus both accept that life is absurd, but, both deal with it in different manners, Sartre ends up confusing his initial philosophy under the influence of 'Marxism', and Camus finds 'Sisyphus', a 'happy' Sisyphus nonetheless.

Traditional philosophers believed that everything has some predefined meaning, an essence, including us humans and this essence is somehow related to a metaphysical reality. Men are born with this essence, and this essence is what defines them throughout their lives. Existentialists like Sartre and Camus and Nietzsche too, weren't able to accept this theory. They asserted that man is not born with an essence or a purpose to fulfil. Men are just born, and as they grow and become familiar with their surrounding they create their own essence. They find a purpose later in life and live for that purpose. They give meaning to their lives themselves by means of their actions and choices. Now, this meaning can be nihilistic, or positive, that depends on the attitude of the person living in a particular situation. A Man's freedom is not an absolute freedom; rather it's a relative, conditional freedom, where he doesn't have a control over the situation he is in, he just has the freedom about what he does with the given situation. What he makes of it.

For Sartre existence strikes suddenly, in a moment of awareness and it is a lot to process. His character Roquentin, in Nausea narrates this experiences in a long passage quoted below;

"I exist. It's sweet, so sweet, so slow. And light: you'd swear that it floats in the air all by itself. It moves. Little brushing movements everywhere which melt and disappear. Gently, gently. There is some frothy water in my mouth. I swallow it, it slides down my throat, it caresses me-and now it is starting up again in my mouth, I have a permanent little pool of whitish water in my mouth- unassuming-touching my tongue. And this pool is me too. And the tongue. And the throat is me.

I see my hand spread out on the table. It is alive- it is me. It opens, the fingers unfold and point. It is lying on its back. It shows me its fat under-belly. It looks like an animal upside down. The fingers are the paws. I amuse myself by making them move about very quickly, like the claws of a crab which has fallen on its back. The crab is dead: the claws curl up and close over the belly of my hand. I see the nails- the only thing in me which isn't alive. And even that isn't sure. My hand turns over, spreads itself out on its belly, and now it is showing me its back. A silvery, somewhat shiny back- you might think it was fish, if it weren't for the red hairs near the knuckles. I feel my hand. It is me, those two animals moving about at the end of my arms. My hand scratches one of its paws with the nail of another paw; I can feel its weight on the table which isn't me. It's long, long, this impression f weight, it doesn't go. There's is no reason why it should go. In the long run, it's unbearable... I withdraw my hand, I put it in my pocket. But straight away, through the material, I feel the warmth of my thigh. I promptly make my hand jump out of my pocket; I let it hang against the back of my chair. Now I feel its weight at the end of my arm. It pulls a little, not very much, gently, softly it exists. I don't press the point: wherever I put it, it will go on existing; I can't suppress it, nor can I suppress the rest of my body, the damp warmth which soils my shirt, nor all this warm fat which turns lazily, as if somebody were stirring it with a spoon, nor all the sensations wandering about inside, coming and going, rising from my side to my armpit or else quietly vegetating, from morning till night, in their usual corner." (Sartre, Nausea 144)[26]

Camus on the other hand did not thought of himself as an existentialist. The problem he dealt with, was that, "is life worth living or not?" At the very beginning of his book 'The myth of Sisyphus', we find the very famous quote of Camus that sums up his philosophical endeavours in a nutshell -

"There is but one truly serious philosophical problem and that is suicide. Judging whether life is worth living or not worth living amounts to answering the fundamental question of philosophy. All the rest –

whether or not the world has three dimensions, whether the mind has nine or twelve categories – comes afterwards." (Camus, The myth of Sisyphus 1)[27]

Camus doesn't deals with the realisation of 'existence'; he deals with what to do next. Sartre presents the essential 'existence' and Camus presents the essential absurdity of that existence.

"At any street corner the feeling of absurdity can strike any man in the face. As it is, in its distressing nudity, in its light without effulgence, it is elusive." (Camus, The myth of Sisyphus 9)[28]

In this flat, absurd existence, what is the role of God? One cannot stubbornly keep claiming that 'God exists because we need him', because that would be irrational. There is a secular moralist approach which Sartre mentions –

"Around 1880, when some French professors attempted to formulate a secular morality, they expressed it more or less in these words: God is a useless and costly hypothesis, so we will do without it. However, if we are to have a morality, a civil society, and a law-abiding world, it is essential that certain values be taken seriously; they must have an a-priori existence ascribed to them. It must be considered mandatory a-priori for people to be honest, not to lie, not to beat their wives, to raise children, and so forth. We therefore will need to do a little more thinking on this subject in order to show that such values exists all the same, and that they are inscribed in an intelligible heaven, even though God does not exist." (Sartre, Existentialism is a Humanism 28)[29]

But Sartre is not comfortable with this attitude. The problem is not as simple this. To find a solution one first has to acknowledge the grandiose of the problem. He further says –

"Existentialists, on the other hand, find it extremely disturbing that God no longer exists, for along with his disappearance goes the possibility of finding values in an intelligible heaven. There could no longer be any a-priori good, since there would be no infinite and perfect consciousness to conceive of it. Nowhere is it written that good exists, that we must be honest or must not lie, since we are on a plane shared only by men. Dostoevsky once wrote: "If God does not exist, everything is permissible". This is the starting point of existentialism. Indeed, everything is permissible if God does not exist, and man is consequently abandoned, for he cannot find anything to rely on – neither within nor without. First, he finds there are no excuses. For it is true that existence precedes essence, we can never explain our actions by reference to a given and immutable human nature. In other words, there is no determinism – man is free, man is freedom. If, however, God does not exist, we will encounter no values or orders that can legitimize our conduct. Thus, we have neither behind us, nor before us, in the luminous realm of values, any means of justification or excuse. That is what I mean when I say that man is condemned to be free: condemned because he did not create himself, yet nonetheless free, because once cast into the world, he is responsible for everything he does." (Sartre, Existentialism is a Humanism 28-29)[30]

Camus too refers to Dostoevsky's character "Kirilov" from 'The possessed' regarding the above mentioned statement –

"To become God is merely to be free on this earth, not to serve an immortal being. Above all, of course, it is drawing all the inferences from that painful independence. If God exists all depends on him and we can do nothing against his will. If he does not exist, everything depends on us. For Kirilov, as for Nietzsche, to kill God is to become god oneself; it is to realize on this earth the eternal life of which the Gospel speaks." (Camus, The myth of Sisyphus 104-105)[31]

But, to Camus, absence of God is not a licence of arbitrary actions, unlike existentialism is accused of occasionally, freedom doesn't have to be an excuse for chaos.

"The certainty of a God giving a meaning to life far surpasses in attractiveness the ability to behave badly with impunity. The choice would not be hard to make. But there is no choice and that is where the bitterness comes in. The absurd does not liberate; it binds. It does not authorize all actions. Everything is permitted does not mean that nothing is forbidden. The absurd merely confers an equivalence on the consequences of those actions. It does not recommend crime, for this would be childish, but it restores to remorse its futility. Likewise, if all experiences are indifferent, that of duty is as legitimate as any other. One can be virtuous through a whim." (Camus, The myth of Sisyphus 65)[32]

The central idea here is, whether or not one chooses to believe in a God, there is a life in front of everyone which he ought to live as perfectly as one could. God and metaphysics are one aspect of life, but apart from that, life itself is beautiful and worth living with all its absurdity. The purpose we seek in life need not be the "perfection", or being united with a supreme power, or something regarding 'after life'.

Life itself might be the purpose of life. For someone who leads a purposeless life, existence is as described by Roquentin, in Nausea, "*... I had appeared by chance, I existed like a stone, a plant, a microbe. My life grew in haphazard way and in all directions*", such an existence in bound to fade into nothingness. But for those who rise up and make a difference whether by means of any form of art or science or humanity, have a meaningful existence, they keep existing at least till mankind manages to survive in the universe.

One can either feel his existence as a disturbing fact or cherish it as a momentary yet beautiful incidence as Camus does –

"Who am I and what can I do – except enter into the movement of the branches and the light, be this ray of sunlight in which my cigarette smolders away, this soft and gentle passion breathing in the air? If I try to reach myself, it is at the heart of this light that I am to be found. And if I try to taste and understand this delicate flavour that contains the secret of the world, it is again myself that I find at the heart of the universe. Myself, that is to say this intense emotion which frees me from my surroundings. Soon, my attention will be filled again with other things and with the world of men. But let me cut out this moment from the cloth of time as other men leave a flower in the pages of a book. In it, they enclose the memory of a walk in which they were touched by love. I also walk through the world, but am caressed by a god. Life is short, and it is a sin to waste one's time. I waste my time all day long, while other people say that I do a great deal. Today is a resting place, and my heart goes out to meet myself." (Camus, Notebooks (1935-1942) 9)[33]

Therefore being in the world, conceives in itself, its own innate beauty and value. Life does not depends for its worth on some religious value. First we exist and then we search for a purpose. That purpose may or may not involve religion and God. The absurdity and depression comes along with the fear of death, the fear of 'non-existence'. That is exactly the point where thought surrenders. That is the point from where either one slips into pessimism and 'dreadful hopelessness' and reach to a conclusion that 'nothing is worth anything', or lulls into mysticism and "hope" that religions provide.

Sartre expresses that feeling of 'dreadful hopelessness' and horror of 'non-existence' –

"Everything was full, everything was active, there was no unaccented beat, everything, even the most imperceptible movement, was made of existence. And all those existents which were busting about the tree came from nowhere and were going nowhere. All of a sudden they existed and then, all of a sudden, they no longer existed; existence has no memory; it retains nothing of what has disappeared; not even a recollection. Existence everywhere, to infinity, superfluous, always and everywhere; existence – which is never limited by anything but existence." (Sartre, Nausea 190)[34]

But to this dreadful hopelessness and horror of non-existence, Camus found a third option. It's to live, and live life to its maximum. He quotes Nietzsche –

"'Art and nothing but art', said Nietzsche; 'we have art in order not to die of the truth'" (Camus, The myth of Sisyphus 90)[35]

Camus asks one to revolt against absurdity and struggle for each moment of happiness. If one has passion for life, one can give it any meaning he wants. This doesn't means that once he chooses a path, things fall into place and life will be all happiness and prosperity, no, one gets thrown away by circumstances again and again, to 'live' means, to stand up and fight back again, with any promise some further ultimate happiness. Happiness has to found in the very process of falling down and standing up again, because that's what life is; an endless loop of falling down and standing up. Camus tells this with the story of Story of Sisyphus, *"The gods had condemned Sisyphus to ceaselessly rolling a rock to the top of a mountain, whence the stone would fall back of its own weight. They had thought with some reason that there is no dreadful punishment than futile and hopeless labour."* (Camus, The myth of Sisyphus 115)[36] But according to Camus, despite the dreadful punishment, Sisyphus's happiness still lies in his own hands, in his passion for life and in his revolt against absurdity of existing without a purpose –

"I leave Sisyphus at the foot of the mountain! One always finds one's burden again. But Sisyphus teaches the higher fidelity that negates the gods and raises rocks. He, too, concludes that all is well. This universe henceforth without a master seems to him neither sterile nor futile. Each atom of that stone, each mineral flake of that night-filled mountain, in itself forms a world. The struggle itself towards the heights is enough to fill a man's heart. One must imagine Sisyphus happy." (Camus, The myth of Sisyphus 119)[37]

Concluding his own philosophy, Camus says;

"Thus, I draw from the absurd three consequences which are my revolt, my freedom and my passion. By the mere activity of consciousness I transform into a rule of life what was an invitation to death- and I refuse suicide." (Camus, The myth of Sisyphus 62)[38]

As per his own personal take on atheism, he had his own way of defining things. He writes in his 'notebook'-

"I often read that I am an atheistic; I hear people speak of my atheism. Yet those words say nothing to me; for me they have no meaning. I do not believe in God and I am not an atheist." (Camus, Notebooks (1951-1959) 112)[39]

Randomness of life existentialism believes in doesn't leaves much scope for any sense behind whatever happens or any controller of the cosmos. But if there is a scope for individual choice of whether or not a person is allowed to indulge in religious faith, it might be of great help to humanity. Different existentialist philosophers deal in different manner with life's absurdity. Sartre surrenders to fatalism considering everything as meaningless (in Nausea), while Camus prefers to challenge this absurdity and fight back.

When one looks death in the eye, there are two ways to live, one to let nothingness consume everything, soak whatever shred of life is remaining in the person, wait with a dead heart for one's body to perish because nothing will last and everything is going to end, or else one can consider his/her remaining days as an opportunity to feel, to live, to know how fortunate one is to have these moments of livelihood amidst this vast emptiness, and how precious every moment is! One can choose anger and a nauseated state of mind or one can embrace beauty and emotions and flavours of life while it lasts. Every form of creativity including religions and mythologies at their origin are inspired by this urge of celebrating what we have, and as their goal they have a yearning in their heart to understand what's after this. This embracing of life, being grateful of what we have and pursuit of what's after this is part of every human existence (at least of those who aware of their existence in existentialist sense). And, each one of us may have our own way regarding the above mentioned. This is what I call an existentialist approach towards religion. One may accept it or one may deny it, that too, would be an existentialist approach, provided the individual making the choice is aware consciously of his choice.

Citation and reference :

1. Sartre, Jean Paul. *Existentialism is Humanism.* Trans. Carol Macombar. New Haven and London: Yale University Press, 2007. P. 22-23.

2. Dostoevsky, Fyodor. *Notes from Underground/The Double.* Trans. Jessie Coulson. London: Penguin Books Ltd., 1972. P. 36.

3. Sartre, Jean Paul. *Existentialism is Humanism.* Trans. Carol Macombar. New Haven and London: Yale University Press, 2007. P. 20.

4. Tolstoy, Leo. *What I Believe.* Trans. Constantine Popoff. New York: William S. Gottsberger Publisher, 1886. P. 24.

5. Someone whose philosophical ideologies are inspired by the work and thoughts of Thomas Acquinas.

6. Maritain, Jacques. *Existence and the Existent.* New York: Garden City Publishing, 1957. P. 80.

7. Ibid. p. 33.

8. Ibid. p. 135-136.

9. Stanford encyclopaedia of philosophy, http://plato.stanford.edu/entries/jaspers/#PhilReli

10. Kaufmann, Walter. *Existentialism from Dostoevsky to Sartre.* Ed. Walter Kaufmann. New York: Penguin Groups, 1975. P. 211-212.

11. Ibid. p. 212.

12. Ibid. p. 22.

13. Ibid. p. 16-17.

14. Ibid. p. 17.

15. Tillich, Paul. *Dynamics of Faith.* New York: Perennial Classics Publication, 2001. P. 48.

16. Ibid.

17. Ibid. p. 55.

18. Kaufmann, Walter, ed. *Existentialism from Dostoevsky to Sartre.* New York: Penguin Groups, 1975. P. 114-115.

19. Nietzsche, Friedrich. *Beyond Good and Evil.* Trans. Walter Kaufmann. Vintage Books Edition. New York: Random House Inc., 1989. P. 71.

20. Nietzsche, Friedrich. *The Antichrist.* Trans. H.L. Mencken. New York: Alfred A. Knopf Inc., !918. p. 12.

21. Kaufmann, Walter, ed. *Existentialism from Dostoevsky to Sartre.* New York: Penguin Groups, 1975. P. 99.

22. Ibid. p. 105-106.

23. Ibid. p. 107.

24. Camus, Albert. *Notebooks(1942-1951).* Trans. Justin O'Brian. Chicago: Alfred A. Knopf Inc., 1965. P. 40.

25. Nietzsche, Friedrich. *Beyond Good and Evil.* Trans. Walter Kaufmann. Vintage Books Edition. New York: Random House Inc., 1989. P. 60.

26. Sartre, Jean Paul. *Nausea.* Trans. Robert Baldick. London: Penguin Books Ltd., 1963. P. 144.

27. Camus, Albert. *The Myth of Sisyphus.* Trans. Justin O' Brien. London: Penguin Books Ltd., 2005. P. 1.

28. Ibid. p. 9.

29. Sartre, Jean Paul. *Existentialism is Humanism.* Trans. Carol Macombar. New Haven and London: Yale University Press, 2007. P. 28.

30. Ibid. p. 28-29.

31. Camus, Albert. *The Myth of Sisyphus.* Trans. Justin O' Brien. London: Penguin Books Ltd., 2005. P. 104-105

32. Ibid. p. 65.

33. Camus, Albert. *Notebooks (1935-1942).*Trans. Philip Thodey. Chicago: Alfred A. Knopf, 1963. P. 9.

34. Sartre, Jean Paul. *Nausea.* Trans. Robert Baldick. London: Penguin Books Ltd., 1963. P. 190.

35. Camus, Albert. *The Myth of Sisyphus.* Trans. Justin O' Brien. London: Penguin Books Ltd., 2005. P. 90.

36. Ibid. p. 115.

37. Ibid. p. 119.

38. Ibid. P. 62.

39. Camus, Albert. *Notebooks(1951-1959).* Trans. Rayn Bloom. Chicago: Ivan R. Dec Inc., 2008. P. 112.

Chapter 4

A critical analysis of Nietzsche's repudiations

The objections Nietzsche has towards religion are expressed in rhetoric manner and are scattered throughout his books, as I have already mentioned he didn't had any systematic way of thinking and writing. They were basically impulsive overflow of emotions. These objections were primarily targeted towards "Christianity", and may be further applied to all 'organised religions'. His major work that projected all his dissatisfaction as well as his expectations with religion is 'Thus spoke Zarathustra', in which he creates a character 'Zarathustra' who resonates a religious preacher who has gained "knowledge" in the solitude of a mountain top and returns to people to share his wisdom. Nietzsche character is more like a parody of the prophets, who in all seriousness hits them with sarcastic yet thought provoking comments. In the process of sharing his wisdom, Nietzsche's Zarathustra goes through a roller-coaster of emotions and thoughts. He finds people who consider him mad, people who find him mystic and people who become his disciple.

By means of Zarathustra, Nietzsche portrays the irony in prophetic religions brilliantly. To the Biblical analogy of 'shepherd', Zarathustra's take is remarkable-

"An insight has come to me: companions I need, living ones- not dead companions and corpses whom I carry with myself wherever I want to. Living companions I need, who follow me because they to follow themselves- wherever I want.

"*An insight has come to me: let Zarathustra speak not to people but to companions. Zarathustra shall not become the shepherd and the dog of a herd.*

"*To lure many away from the herd, for that I have come. The people and the herd shall be angry with me: Zarathustra wants to be called a robber by the shepherds.*

"*Shepherds, I say; but they call themselves the good and the just. Shepherds, I say; but they call themselves believer in true faith.*

"*Behold the good and the just! Whom do they hate most? The man who breaks their tables of value, the breaker, the law breaker; yet he is the creator.*

"*Behold the believers of all faiths! Whom do they hate most? The man who breaks their tables of values, the breaker, the lawbreaker; yet he is the creator.*

"*Companions, the creator seeks, not corpses, not herds and believers. Fellow creators, the creator seeks- those who write new values to the tablets. Companions the creator seeks and fellow harvesters; for everything about him is ripe for the harvest. But he lacks a hundred sickles: so he plucks ears and is annoyed. Companions, the creator seeks, and such as know how to whet their sickles. Destroyers they will be called, and despisers of good and evil. But they are the harvesters and those who celebrate. Fellow creators, Zarathustra seeks, fellow harvesters and fellow celebrants: what are herds and shepherds and corpses to him?*" (F. Nietzsche, Thus Spoke Zarathustra 2)[1]

Nietzsche was trying to shake the consciousness of people, so that they might think for themselves. Unlike 'religion', he was not interested in regulating a mindless herd. 'Followers', he considered weak, as they don't contribute anything to the world. And what good is a religion which promotes weakness, which demands **not to think.** In Ecce-homo he writes about his atheism directly, claiming that it's the only intellectual possibility. Any high-spirited intellectual cannot bow down to the prohibition over asking questions.

"Atheism is not at all familiar to me as a result, still less as an event: it is self-evident to me from instinct. I am too curious, too dubious, too high-spirited to content myself with a rough-and-ready answered is a rough-and-ready answer, an indelicacy against us thinkers – basically even just a rough- and-ready prohibition on us: you shall not think!" (F. Nietzsche, Ecce Homo 19)[2]

It is important to understand that Nietzsche does not refute metaphysical statements like analytical philosophers refute them. A notable example of analytical argument regarding worthlessness of religious statements from Tractatus Logico-Philosophicus, is –

"Skeptism is not irrefutable but obviously non-sensical when it tries to raise doubts where no questions can be asked.

For doubt can exist only where a question exists, a question only when an answer exists and an answer only where something can be said."[3]

Nietzsche doesn't refute metaphysical statements that way, or by calling them pseudo-statements like Carnap does. His ground of refuting them is rather pragmatic. His objections range from a variety of childlike impulses to deep psychological analysis. In his preface for the second edition of Gay Science, Nietzsche reports a very light and satirical objection towards God –

"We no longer believe that truth remains truth when the veils are withdrawn; we have lived too much to believe this. Today we consider it a matter of decency not to wish to see everything naked, or to be present at everything or to understand and "know" everything.

"Is it true that God is present everywhere?" a little girl asked her mother: "I think that's indecent" – a hint for philosophers! One should have more respect for the bashfulness with which the nature has hidden behind riddles and iridescent uncertainties. Perhaps truth is a woman who has reasons for not letting us see her reasons?" (F. Nietzsche, The Gay Science 38)[4]

While above mentioned paragraph might not be taken as a serious argument about religious theories of concept of God, it does indicates towards a subtle manner of letting deeper realities be as they are and not meddling with the bigger natural phenomenon's which are beyond our understanding. We most certainly don't need to superimpose ideas over ideas to natural realities. It's just an unnecessary endeavour. Religion, especially how it turned out to be, is an unnecessary endeavour. For what does it matter whether the world we live in is 'appearance' or 'reality'? And what does it matters even if there actually is something beyond our senses! Because the bottom line is we can only play our part within the limits of our body and then we have to perish, and so will this planet, and so will this galaxy, and who knows where it ends! Even if we accept as Indian Vedas and mystics tells us, that all this is a dream, what option do we have other than kept on dreaming? Because whatever mystical universal spirit they hope us to unite with after waking up, it doesn't promises the existence of individual consciousness and therefore doesn't provides any consolation for those who value individual existence. To Nietzsche, there is no 'objective reality' behind this dream, there is no essence and even if one knows he is dreaming, he would rather prefer the continuation of the dream.

"The consciousness of appearance – How wonderful and new and yet how gruesome and ironic I find my position vis-a-vis the whole existence in the light of my insight! I have discovered for myself that the human and animal past, indeed the whole primal age and past of all sentient being continues in me to invent, to love, to hate, and to infer. I suddenly woke up in the midst of in the midst of this dream but only to the consciousness that I am dreaming and that I must go on dreaming lest I perish – as a somnambulist must go on dreaming lest he fall. What is the appearance for me now? Certainly not the opposite of some essence: What could I say about any essence except to name the attributes of its appearance! Certainly not a dead mask that ne could place on an unknown x or remove from it!

Appearance is for me that which lives and is effective and goes so far in its self-mockery that it makes me feel that this is appearance and will-o-the wisp and dance of spirits and noting more – that among all these dreamers, I, too, who "know" am dancing my dance; that the knower is a means for prolonging the earthly dance and thus belongs to the masters of ceremony of existence; and that the sublime consistency and the interrelatedness of all knowledge perhaps is and will be the highest means to preserve the universality of dreaming and the mutual comprehension of all dreamers and thus also the mutual comprehension of all dreamers and thus also the continuation of the dream." (F. Nietzsche, The Gay Science 116)[5]

Kauffman further explains the passage in his footnote of the same –

"In other words, the world of our experience is shaped by our pre-rational past and may be likened to a dream. But even when we realize how the world of our experience lacks objectivity and independent reality, we still "must go on dreaming". What we experience is "appearance"; but there is no "essence" behind it that is somehow falsified. Appearance is not a mask that we might hope to remove from the face of an unknown x. There is no objective reality, no-thing-in-itself; there is only appearance in one or another perspective." (F. Nietzsche, The Gay Science 116)[6]

What mankind has to deal with is the 'appearance'; hence, what mankind actually needs is not some superficial theory about how world was created or what happens after life, rather how to say 'yes' to this 'life'.

"When the centre of gravity of life is placed, not in life itself, but in "the beyond" – in nothingness – then one has taken away its centre of gravity altogether." (F. Nietzsche, The Antichrist 22)[7]

Thus, his first major objection towards religion was the search for 'beyond'.

His second repudiation was regarding the emphasis on 'obeying', 'prohibition on asking questions' and 'faith'. According to him, those are the factors associated with a cultural decline as culture thrives on diversity of independent thinking, and in a godless world, what adds value to life is art, music and culture. Fear or indifference regarding any kind of change will only cause friction in the natural growth of humanity. Systems that promote this fear are unlikely to survive because they will sooner or later lose their worth. Religion, especially prophetic religion forces man to 'obey', and 'follow' what has been said without leaving any scope for new ideas to develop and there begins the decline. I would like to take another excerpt from 'The Antichrist' –

"...under the hand of the Jewish priesthood the great age of Israel became an age of decline; the Exile, with its long series of misfortunes, was transformed into a punishment for that great age – during which priests had not yet come into existence. Out of the powerful yet wholly free heroes of Israel's history they fashioned, according to their changing needs, either wretched bigots and hypocrites or men entirely "godless". They reduced every great event to the idiotic formula: "obedient or disobedient to God." – They went a step further: the "will of God" (in other words some means necessary for preserving the power of the priests) had to be determined – and to this end they had to have a "revelation". In plain English, a gigantic literary fraud had to be perpetrated, and "holy scriptures" had to be concocted – and so, with the utmost hierarchical pomp, and days of penance and much lamentation over the long days of "sin" now ended, they were duly published." (F. Nietzsche, The Antichrist 15)[8]

What makes 'man' superior to animals is his ability to reason. That is the primary reason how all the religions came into existence in the first place, as we have discussed before. But it's ironical how these religions turned opposite to this very primary nature of mankind. Religion uses 'faith' as its 'tool', which is not only anti-intellectual but also dangerous because it does not require any 'objective truth' to act upon. Faith itself is enough. And its danger is twofold; first it blocks every possibility of further progress, and second, if placed in wrong thing or wrong people, it can cause destruction beyond imagination. The illogical structure of the arguments based on faith can be seen in the following example of 'The Koran' (oxford world classics) –

"How do you disbelieve in God, seeing you were dead and he gave you life, then He shall make you dead, then He shall give you life, then unto Him you shall be returned?" (4)[9]

Also, Koran does not speaks only on behalf of Muslims, but everyone who believes in God –

"Surely they that believe, and those of Jewry, and the Christians, and those Sabaeans, whoso believes in God and the Last Day, and works righteousness – their wage awaits them with their Lord, and no fear shall be on them, neither shall they sorrow." (8)[10]

Paragraphs resonating same ideas can be found in every religious text whatsoever. The people having these religious arguments don't bother about making sense. These arguments don't support any truth; instead they couldn't care any less about the 'truth'. That is what makes these arguments based on 'faith' unacceptable to Nietzsche –

"It is then a matter of acquiring the view of God, world, and atonement in which one can feel most comfortable? Is it not, rather, true that for the true researcher the result for his research is of no account at all? Do we in our investigations, search for tranquillity, peace, happiness? No – only for the truth, even if it were to be frightening and ugly.

One last remaining question. If we had believed since youth that all salvation came not from Jesus but from another – say, from Mohammad – is it not certain that we would have enjoyed the same blessings? To be sure, faith alone gives blessing, not the objective which stands behind the faith. I write this to you, dear Lisbeth, only in order to counter the most usual proofs of believing people, who invoke the evidence of their inner experiences and deduce from it the infallibility of their faith. Every true faith is indeed infallible; it performs what the believing person hopes to find in it, but it does not offer the least support for the establishing of an objective truth.

Here the ways of men divide. If you want to achieve peace of mind and happiness, then have faith; if you want to be a disciple of truth, then search.

Between, there are many halfway positions. But it all depends on the principal aim." (F. Nietzsche, Selected letters of Friedrich Nietzsche 7)[11]

His third objection towards Religions, especially Christianity is that, they declare every natural human instinct as 'immoral' or 'sin'. Whether it is the desire for power, rage, self-love, desire to fulfil the appetite of senses, may t be food, comfort or sexual pleasure. According to Nietzsche, any species flourish when it enhances its natural abilities. An organism is defined by its biological qualities. Restraining them creates a hindrance in development of a mankind.

"We should not deck out and embellish Christianity: it has waged a war to the death against this higher type of man, it has put all the deepest instincts of this type under its ban, it has developed its concept of evil, of the Evil One himself, out of these instincts – the strong man as the typical reprobate, the "outcast among men". Christianity has taken the part of all the week, the low, the botched; it has made an ideal out of antagonism to all the self-preservative instincts of sound life; it has corrupted even the faculties of those natures that are intellectually most vigorous, by representing the highest intellectual values as sinful, as misleading, as full of temptation. The most lamentable example: the corruption of Pascal, who believed that his intellect had been destroyed by original sin, whereas it was actually destroyed by Christianity!" (F. Nietzsche, The Antichrist 8)[12]

Further he explains this point in Beyond Good and Evil;

"There is no other way: the feelings of devotion, self-sacrifice for one's neighbour, the whole morality of self-denial must be questioned mercilessly and taken to the court – no less than the aesthetics of contemplation devoid of all interest" which is used today as seductive guise for the emasculation of art, to give it a good conscience. There is too much charm and sugar in these feelings of *"for others"*, *"not for*

myself" for us not to need to become doubly suspicious at this point and to ask: "are these not perhaps – seductions?"

That they please – those who have them and those who enjoy their fruits, and also the mere spectator – this does not yet constitute an argument in their favour but rather invites caution. So let us be cautious. (F. Nietzsche 45)[13]

However, it's important to understand here that when Nietzsche speaks for promoting man's natural instincts and love of 'self', he does not means to promote 'agony' and 'vengeance'. He is not encouraging in any manner that those who have power should torment the weak or rule over them. He has been widely misunderstood regarding this point. Yes, he does believes in a sort of 'aristocratic individualism' i.e. some people are superior in their intellectual and physical capabilities than others. What he says again and again is that those who are stronger should not be restrained or confined in order to spare the sentiments of the weak. This attitude based on 'pity' towards the weak, might satisfy the emotions of the herd, but is not in favour of the overall development of mankind. Every individual must use his maximum potential and everyone must struggle to attain his best so that the whole human race might reach to its height and in order to achieve this bigger goal we have to let go of the collateral damage.

When looking from a sociological point, this might seem a bit extreme to many thinkers, as humanitarian goals have always been to extend their efforts to the socially and financially weak and bring them to the central stream of life. We live in a relative universe where everything and everyone is correlated. If we want to survive for long as race, we cannot completely abandon the soft sentiments Nietzsche criticizes. But this too should be taken into account that these sentiments do not develop a tendency of unnecessary dependency, a permanent paralyses of will power to make an extra effort, a reluctance of giving up the favour even if not needed.

Anyhow, all Nietzsche is asking for is a healthy competition without the weak sentiments of 'pity' and 'sacrifice'. Especially the Christian concept of sacrifice promoted by the example of the sacrifice of Jesus seems unreasonable and unfair to him. It just sets wrong example regarding 'justice'. But he never promoted 'toxic' emotions. In Ecce Homo he says –

"And nothing burns you up faster than the emotions of resentment. Anger, sickly vulnerability, powerlessness to take revenge, the lust, the thirst for revenge, every kind of poisonous troublemaking – for the exhausted this is certainly the most detrimental way of reacting: it brings on a rapid consumption of nervous strength, a sickly intensification of harmful excretions, for example of bile in the stomach. For the invalid, resentment is the absolute forbidden – his evil: unfortunately his most natural inclination, too. – This is what that profound physiologist Buddha understood. His 'religion', which ought rather to be called a hygiene so as not to conflate it with such wretched things as Christianity, made its effects conditional on defeating resentment: liberating the soul from that – first step towards recovery. 'Not through enmity does enmity come to an end; enmity comes to an end through friendship': this stands at the

beginning of Buddha's teaching – this is not morality speaking, but physiology." (F. Nietzsche, Ecce Homo 14)[14]

Furthermore, what Nietzsche hates not only in Christianity, but in every major religion, is the concept of 'self-deceit'. Almost every religion makes people 'delusional'. People tend to seek imaginary solutions of real problems. Out of this grand enterprise called 'Religion' people are not actually getting anything more than what is offered through 'drugs' or 'alcohol'. (That is the same reason why Nietzsche hates alcohol too).

"Under Christianity neither morality nor religion has any point of contact with actuality. It offers purely imaginary causes ("God", "soul", "ego", "spirit", "free will" – or even "unfree"), and purely imaginary effects ("sin", "salvation", "grace", "punishment", "forgiveness of sins"). Intercourse between imaginary beings ("God", "spirits", "souls"); an imaginary natural history (anthropocentric; a total denial of the concept of natural causes); an imaginary psychology (misunderstandings of self, misinterpretations of agreeable or disagreeable general feelings – for example, of the states of the nervus sympathicus with the help of the sign language of religio-ethical balderdash – "repentence", "pangs of conscience", "temptation by the devil", "the presence of God); an imaginary teleology (the "kingdom of God", "the last judgement", "eternal life"). – This purely fictitious world, greatly to its disadvantage, is to be differentiated from the world of dreams; the later at least reflects reality, whereas the former falsifies it, cheapens it and denies it. Once the concept of "nature" had been opposed to the concept of "God", the word "natural" necessarily took on the meaning of "abominabe" – the whole of that fictitious world has its

sources in hatred of the natural (- the real! -), and is no more than evidence of a profound uneasiness in the presence of reality. This explains everything. Who alone has any reason for living his way out of reality? The man who suffers under it. But to suffer from reality one must be a botched reality. The preponderance of pains over pleasures is the cause of this fictitious morality and religion: but such a preponderance also supplies the formula for decadence." (F. Nietzsche, The Antichrist 10-11)[15]

He compares the state of a religious person with a person in love –

" – Love is the state in which an sees things most decidedly as they are not. The force of illusion reaches its highest here, and so does the capacity for sweetening, for transfiguring. When a man is in love he endures more than at any other time; he submits to anything. The problem was to devise a religion which would allow one to love: by this means the worst that life has to offer is overcome – it is scarcely even noticed." (F. Nietzsche, The Antichrist 13)[16]

Hence, without being aware of what people are adhering to, they act, as if hypnotised by the imaginary idea of far-away-happiness. They endure everything possible in the false expectation of the 'promised world'. This whole facade of a farther perfect world after life revolves around the idea of a "soul" or "pure spirit" which Nietzsche ridicules as "pure stupidity".

4.1 "Pure Spirit" or "Pure stupidity"

"Formerly it was thought that man's consciousness, his "spirit", offered evidence of his high origin, his divinity. That he might be perfected, he was advised, tortoise-like, to draw his senses in, to have no traffic with earthly things, to shuffle off his mortal coil – then only the important part of him, the "pure spirit", would remain. Here again we have thought out the thing better: to us consciousness, or "the spirit", appears as a symptom of a relative imperfection of the organism, as an experiment, a groping, a misunderstanding, as an affliction which uses up nervous force unnecessarily – we deny that anything can be done perfectly so long as it is done consciously. The "pure spirit" is a piece of pure stupidity: take away the nervous system and the senses, the so called "mortal shell", and the rest is miscalculation – that is all." (F. Nietzsche, The Antichrist 10)[17]

However blunt above passage may seem, it contains the fundamental idea of Nietzsche's philosophy regarding the concept of spirit. Among the objections mentioned in previous chapter, most important one is the problem of 'spirit' or 'soul' or 'consciousness' and how it plays the major role in our weakness regarding the matters of religion. There is not any universally true definition of 'soul' or 'spirit'. Some believe it to be an entity present somewhere in the body, others call it the essence of one's being. The struggle of mind-body problem is age old in history of philosophy. Almost every philosopher has his own take on 'soul'. Eastern philosophers consider it as an individual manifestation of the 'universal energy' or 'Brahman'. Cartesian idea is of 'thinking-self' which is different from body. Descartes tried to explain the relationship of this 'self' with body by means of a gland called 'pineal-gland', which was a disastrous attempt and compromised the consistency of Descartes philosophy. Prior to Descartes, Aristotle believed soul to be NOT an entity, but an aspect of any natural entity, a potentiality. He even classified the level of 'soul' gradually increasing from plant-level to animal-level and then human-level. One can understand Aristotle's use of term 'soul' as 'level of consciousness' or 'rational-ability'.

Nietzsche, however, has a critical attitude to the concept of 'soul'. He does not blindly believe that there has to be a 'soul' which survives after the body perishes, but he doesn't refuse the concept of a 'soul' altogether. He accepts it as a considerable hypothesis which needs further investigation. If philosophers will be open to new ideas regarding the concept of 'soul', it may be valuable in solving the metaphysical problem–

"One must, however, go still further, and also declare war, relentless war unto death, against the "atomisticneed" which still leads a dangerous afterlife in places where no one suspects it, just like the more celebrated "metaphysical need": one must also, first of all, give the finishing stroke to that other and more calamitous atomism which Christianity has taught best and longest, the soul atomism. Let it be permitted to designate by this expression the belief which regards the soul as something indestructible, eternal, indivisible, as a monad, as an atomon: this belief ought to be expelled from science! Between ourselves, it is not at all necessary to get rid of "the soul" at the same time, and thus to renounce one of the most ancient and venerable hypothesis- as happens frequently to clumsy naturalists who can hardly touch on "the

soul" without immediately losing it. But the way is open for new versions and refinements of the soul-hypothesis; and such conceptions as "mortal soul", and "soul as subjective multiplicity" and "soul as social structure of the drives and affects", wants henceforth to have citizens' right in science. When the new psychologist puts an end to the superstitions which have so far flourished with almost tropical luxuriance around the idea of the soul, he practically exiles himself to a new desert and a new suspicion – it is possible that the older psychologist had a merrier and more comfortable time of it; eventually, however, he finds that precisely thereby he also condemns himself to invention – and – who knows? –perhaps to discovery. " (F. Nietzsche 20-21)[18]

Therefore, instead of being lured to a romanticized idea of 'soul', Nietzsche hope for something pragmatic and realistic, something more relatable. As long as the concept of soul is needed for the masses to function, they will keep finding an excuse to believe in it. But the well-known psychological tendency of humans to 'glorify' what is difficult and opposite to natural tendencies, man has devised an idea of 'spirit' which is 'abstract' and 'pure'. This 'pure spirit' has been established as a 'goal' and to achieve this goal one has to overcome the natural urges of the body. Thus, 'boy' which is very real is despised over the superficial idea of 'pure spirit'. This is where 'soul' becomes dangerous. What should be considered as a 'soul', how it functions or what is its form is another area of study, to which Nietzsche too agrees, but negation of 'body' and of 'instincts', in order to satisfy a superficial hypothesis of soul is unacceptable, in fact 'stupid' in Nietzsche's words. In his Zarathustra, he calls out to the 'Despisers of the body' –

"I want to speak to the despisers of the body. I would not have them learn and teach differently, but merely say farewell to their own bodies – and thus become silent.

"Body am I, and Soul" – Thus speaks the child. And should one not speak like children?

But the awakened and knowing say: body am I entirely, and nothing else; and soul is only a word for something about the body.

The body is a great reason, a plurality with one sense, a war and a peace, a herd and a shepherd. An instrument of your body is also your little reason, my brother, which you call "spirit" – a little instrument and toy of your great reason.

"I", you say, and are proud of the word. But greater is that in which you do not wish to have faith – your body and its great reason: that does not say "I", but does "I".

What the sense feels, what the spirit knows, never has its end in itself. But sense and spirit would persuade you that they are the end of all things: that is how vain they are. Instruments and toys are sense and spirit: behind them still lies the self. The self also seeks with the eyes of the senses; it also listens with the ears of the spirit. Always the self listens and seeks: it compares, overpowers, conquers, destroys. It controls, and it is in control of the ego too.

Behind your thoughts and feelings, my brother, there stands a mighty ruler, an unknown sage – whose name is self. In your body he dwells; he is your body.

There is more reason in your body than in your best wisdom. And who knows why your body needs precisely your best wisdom?

Your self laughs at your ego and at its bold leaps. "what are these leaps and flights of thought to me?" it says to itself. "A detour to my end. I am the leading strings of the ego and the prompter of its concepts."

The self says to the ego, "Feel pain here!" Then the ego suffers and thinks how it might suffer no more – and that is why it is made to think.

The self says to the ego, "Feel pleasure here!" Then the ego is pleased and thinks how it might often be pleased again – and that is why it is made to think.

I want to speak to the despisers of the body. It is their respect that begets their contempt. What is it that created respect and contempt and worth and will? The creative self created respect and contempt; it created pleasure and pain. The creative body created the spirit as a hand for its will.

Even in your folly and contempt, you despisers of the body, you serve your self. I say unto you: your self itself wants to die and turns away from life. It is no longer capable of what it would do above all else: to create beyond itself. That is what it would do above all else, that is its fervent wish.

But now it is too late for it to do this: so your self wants to go under. O despisers of the body. Your self wants to go under, and that is why you have become despisers of the body! For you are no longer able to create beyond yourselves.

And that is why you are angry with life and the earth. An unconscious envy speaks out of the squint-eyed glance of your contempt.

I shall not go your way, O despisers of the body! You are bridge to the overman!

Thus spoke Zarathustra." (F. Nietzsche, Thus Spoke Zarathustra 34-35)[19]

We sure have a creative freedom regarding the form of essence of the being. But whatever theory we choose, it should be essentially life furthering, otherwise it's of no use. It is worth keeping in mind that, whatever Nietzsche speaks on 'soul', 'God', 'religion' or 'metaphysics', he only speaks of it as 'one more hypothesis', a 'theory' created by human mind in order to survive, a mere philosophical standpoint to satisfy the psyche of man. He never claims it to be objectively 'true'. One may choose whichever theory he feels comfortable in, but his believing so doesn't makes anything 'true'. Problem arises when one theory is believed by the "mass" to be true and no further investigation regarding the matter is allowed. Whatever we have in the name of 'soul', 'spirit', 'God' or religion; everything, every single concept is a result of human creativity and to banish human creativity in order to protect these concepts is not only 'stupid', it is unfortunate.

Relationship between body and soul cannot be understood in terms of subject and predicate, neither can they be understood as contradictory entities. Even if there is a soul different than the body, the most we can assume is that they both function as a unit. At least that is how one experiences them.

"For, formerly, one believed in "the soul" as one believed in grammar and the grammatical subject: one said, "I" is the condition, "think" is the predicate and conditioned – thinking is an activity to which thought must supply a subject as cause. The one tried with admirable perseverance and cunning to get out of this net – and asked whether the opposite might not be the case: "think" the condition, "I" the conditioned; "I" in that case only a synthesis which is made by thinking. " (F. Nietzsche 67)[20]

Finally the most apt point that Nietzsche makes, and needs to be taken seriously is that, why must one try assign a deeper meaning to everything that is happening. What good can come out of denying what is in front of the eyes and struggling to find some hidden faraway reality? Even if there is a reality underneath all this appearance, what difference does it makes in the quality of life. In the end, what man really needs is a way to survive the appearance he perceives by means of his senses.

This thought provoking aphorism quoted below, from Beyond Good and evil, sums up the idea–

"Whatever philosophical standpoint one may adopt today, from every point of view the erroneousness of the world in which we think we live is the surest and firmest fact that we can lay eyes on: we find reasons upon reason for it which would like to lure us to hypothesis concerning deceptive principle in "the essence of things". But whoever holds our thinking itself, "the spirit", in other words, responsible for the falseness

of the world – an honourable way out which is chosen by every conscious or unconscious advocates dei – whoever takes this world, along with space, time, form, movement, to be falsely inferred – anyone like that would at least have ample reason to learn to be suspicious at long last of all thinking. Wouldn't thinking have put over on us the biggest hoax yet? And what warrant would there be that it would not continue to do what it has always done?

In all seriousness: the innocence of our thinkers is somehow touching and evoke reverence, when today they still step before consciousness with the request that it should please give them honest answers; for example, whether it is "real", and why it so resolutely keeps the external world at a distance, and other questions of that kind. The faith in "immediate certainties' is moral naivete that reflects honour on us philosophers; but – after all we should not be "merely moral" men. Apart from morality, this faith is a stupidity that reflects little honour on us. In bourgeois life every present suspicion may be considered a sign of "bad character" and hence belong among the things imprudent; here among us, beyond the bourgeois world and its Yes and No – what should prevent us from being imprudent and saying: a philosopher has nothing less than a right to "bad character", as the being who has so far always been fooled best on earth; he has a duty to suspicion today, to squint maliciously out of every abyss of suspicion.

Forgive me the joke of this gloomy grimace and trope; for I myself have learned long ago to think differently, to estimate differently with regard to deceiving and being deceived. Why not? It is no more than a moral prejudice that truth is worth more than mere appearance; it is even the worst proved assumption there is in the world. Let at least this much be admitted: there would be no life at all if not on the basis of perspective estimates and appearances; and if, with the virtuous enthusiasm and clumsiness of some philosophers, one wanted to abolish the "apparent world" altogether – well, supposing you could do that, at least nothing would be left of your "truth" either. Indeed, what forces us at all to suppose that there is an essential opposition of "true" and "false"? Is it not sufficient to assume degrees of apparentness and, as it were, lighter and darker shadows and shades of appearance – different "values", to the language of painters? Why couldn't the world that concerns us be a fiction? And if somebody asked, "but to a fiction there surely belongs an author?" - couldn't one answer simply: why? Doesn't this "belongs" perhaps belong to the fiction too? Is it not permitted to be a bit ironical about the subject no less than the predicate and object? Shouldn't philosophers be permitted to rise above faith in grammar? All due respect for governesses – but hasn't the time come for philosophy to renounce the faith of governesses?" (F. Nietzsche 45-47)[21]

4.2 The Gadfly

The term 'gadfly' has been used in ancient literature over and again, including Shakespeare's "Antony and Cleopatra". Gradually the term gained a metaphorical value for someone who provokes people to change their state of intellectual slumber by attacking them continuously and making them uncomfortable in the passive state they are. In this sense, Plato used this term in his 'Apology', where Socrates has been said to use the term for himself as someone who irritates the society for a greater good. As we all know, Socrates used to ask uncomfortable offensive questions from common people as well as authorities to lead them towards better answers. Same is the role of Nietzsche's philosophy where philosophers and thinkers are concerned. He acts as a bitter medicine, as someone who is not afraid to look bad in order to stir up the conscious of common people. He used a deconstructive philosophy by challenging his predecessors and the commonly accepted ideas regarded as axioms i.e. self-evident truth.

Men have grown too comfortable in their theories, and they are reluctant to acknowledge the fact that the world is no longer the place it once used to be. The theories regarding 'God' and lifestyle dictated by religions have grown irrelevant. The paradigm shift from medieval era to modernism and from modernism to post modernism is cry for attention towards this gradual irrelevance of 'God' and 'religion' in the orthodox sense. This fact is even more undeniable now than Nietzsche's time period. Nietzsche was a visionary to see this truth long before. The irrelevance of 'God' or in Nietzsche words, the 'death of God' is an unfortunate yet inevitable occurrence. People have to accept it first in order to move forward towards the solution. But men prefer a state of denial; they prefer the ghostly shadows of false hopes than face the reality–

"After Buddha was dead, his shadow was still shown for centuries in a cave – a tremendous, gruesome shadow. God is dead; but given the way of men, there may still be caves for thousands of years in which his shadow will be shown. – And we – we still have to vanquish his shadow, too." (F. Nietzsche, The Gay Science 167)[22]

To face the fact, they need a hard push, a continuous sting, and an annoying voice repeatedly telling them about the falseness of their perfect world. That's what Nietzsche does. When he attempts to remove God out of the picture, he is well aware that it will create a void. He realizes what he is asking to give up, and it is hard for him too. He has spent his whole intellectual life carrying the weight of his choice. His words are harsh and hurtful, but it's a requirement if one aims for the thick and passive consciousness of the masses, whose numbness only stirs when their fragile religious sentiments are targeted. He attacks at people's ego, calls them dumb and stupid, on occasions 'blockheads' for adhering without doubting, he wants them to be sceptical –

"I keep having the same experience and keep resisting it every time. I do not want to believe it although it is palpable: the great majority of people lack an intellectual conscience. Indeed, it has often seemed to me as if anyone calling for an intellectual conscience were as lonely in the most densely populated cities as if he were in a desert. Everybody looks at you with strange eyes and goes right on handling his scales,

calling this good and that evil. Nobody even blushes when you intimate that their weights are under-weight; nor do people feel outraged; they merely laugh at their doubts. I mean: the great majority of people does not consider it contemptible to believe this or that and live accordingly, without first having given themselves an account of the final and most certain reasons pro and con, and without even troubling themselves about such reasons afterward: the most gifted men and the noblest women still belong to this "great majority". But what is goodheartedness, refinement or genius to me, when the person who has these virtues tolerates slack feelings in his faith and judgements and when he does not account the desire for certainty as his inmost craving and deepest distress – as that which separates the higher human beings from the lower." (F. Nietzsche, The Gay Science 76)[23]

Furthermore, he says again and again that 'morality' is overrated. Philosophers have a right to 'bad character'. He has to give up the desire of being accepted by the mass. He sure will be hated and repudiated by the men of his time, because he will be damaging their state of inertia. Because he will be disturbing their comfort zone, as did Galileo, as did Socrates, as did Freud, Darwin or Marx. He gladly accepted the task. In a letter to Franz Overbeck on February 5, 1888, he writes –

"I am hard at work too; and the outlines of an unquestionably immense task before me are emerging more and more clearly from the mists. There were dark moments meanwhile, whose days and nights when I did not know any longer how to go on living and when a black despair attacked me, worse than I have ever known before. Nevertheless I know that I cannot escape by going backward or to the right or to the left. I

have o choice. This logic alone is now keeping me going; seen from any other side, my state is untenable and so painful so as to be a torture. My latest books showed something of this; in this state of a bow strung to the highest possible tension any emotion is good for one, provided it is a violent emotion. No more "beautiful things" are to be expected of me: no more than one should expect a suffering and starving animal to attack its prey gracefully. The perpetual lack of a really refreshing and healing human love, the absurd isolation which it entails, making almost any residue of a connection with people merely something that wounds one – that is all very bad indeed and right only in itself, having the right to be necessary." (F. Nietzsche, Selected letters of Friedrich Nietzsche 282)[24]

He spoke against every softness, against everything 'pious' and 'unquestionable', everything that has been made too pure to be reached by humans. He called it **philosophizing with a hammer**, to which Rose Pfeffer points out –

"But having led, in his analysis of nihilism, to a state of negativity and emptiness, Nietzsche now has the task of finding "the exit and hole through which one arrives at something", to construct a new culture that can lead mankind out of the crisis of nihilism. "How to philosophize with a hammer" is the subtitle of The Twilights of the Idols. But the hammer is not only a tool of destruction; it is also an instrument of reconstruction." (Pfeffer 79)[25]

But what is Nietzsche's input towards reconstruction? Primary criticism Nietzsche faces is that his attempt is not wholesome and well constructed and he keeps on attacking without proposing a solution. He points out to the contradictions and hypocrisy of the status-quo, he tells what is wrong with the world, but he doesn't tell what should be instead. But maybe it is not always possible for the same person to bear the solution in mind while pointing towards the problem. The need to find a solution prior to putting forward the problem makes one vulnerable and weak. The urgency of finding a replacement beforehand takes away the sharpness, the force, the fearlessness of an honest scrutiny. Someone scared of what he might lose, someone who thinks of the consequences, someone responsible enough to realize the need of a system before questioning the status-quo, in order to avoid chaos will always hesitate. This hurry for finding a solution in the past has resulted in absurd answers. This is a disappointment that fundamental questions of existential importance, which need a deeper understanding and through going analysis are wasted by the rush of their thinkers. History of philosophy, both of west and of orient is filled with attempts to develop either metaphysics that suits their epistemology or provide epistemology that satisfies their metaphysics. Both are unfortunate because the sort of philosophy which, in order to provide theoretically correct answers, loses touch with reality, does no good to the intellectual, instead creates unnecessary diversions.

Nietzsche is irresponsible, blunt and carefree. He is in revolt with everything he finds contradictory and/or hypocrite but he is not in a hurry to provide theoretically correct answers. He doesn't care for the consequences and hence is not reluctant to speak what is in his mind. This is what makes him perfect for the task. If one honestly wants to find obvious loopholes and faults in the traditions we so proudly uphold, one just needs to read Nietzsche. As per the solutions of the problem he raises, we have a whole generation of thinkers to find innovative ideas coherent with the changing world.

However, Nietzsche does propose that, one can always turn towards art, literature and music for spiritual elevation and peace of mind, instead of musing themselves with superficial concepts like 'religion'. That's the only possible way to lead a life of quality. At least those who have the subtle ability to understand art must take a stand for it. Although it is the hard truth that value of art, philosophy and literature is for few, but those few must not succumb to masses. If the fate of philosophers and artists were to be decided by 'many', the pages of books will be used to wipe dust and sell snacks. Many should not have the authority over a thinker or artist. Neither should philosophy be used to serve political agendas. According to Nietzsche, art for the sake of art, philosophy for the sake of philosophy, an unbiased contemplation, an authentic music, an overwhelming dance can be perfectly fine replacement for religion.

Citation and References :

1. Nietzsche, Friedrich. *Thus Spoke Zarathustra.* Trans. Walter Kaufmann. Modern Library edition. New York: Random House USA, 1995. P. 2.
2. Nietzsche, Friedrich. *Ecce Homo.* Trans. Duncun Large. New York: Oxford University Press. 2007. P. 19.
3. Tractatus Logico-Philosophicus, 51, Ludwig Wittginstien.

4. Nietzsche, Friedrich. *The Gay Science.* Trans. Walter Kaufmann. Vintage Books edition. New York: Random House Publication, 1974. P. 38.

5. Ibid. p. 116.

6. Ibid.

7. Nietzsche, Friedrich. *The Antichrist.* Trans. H. L. Mencken. New York: Alfred A. Knopf Inc., 1918. P. 22.

8. Ibid. p. 15.

9. *The Koran.* New York: Oxford University Press, 2008. P. 4.

10. Ibid. p. 8.

11. Nietzsche, Friedrich. *Selected Letters of Friedrich Nietzsche.* Ed. Christopher Middleton. Indianapolis: Hackett Publishing Company, Inc., 1918. P. 7.

12. Nietzsche, Friedrich. *The Antichrist.* Trans. H. L. Mencken. New York: Alfred A. Knopf Inc., 1918. P. 8.

13. Nietzsche, Friedrich. *Beyond Good and Evil.* Trans. Walter Kaufmann. Vintage Books Edition. New York: Random House Inc., 1989. P. 45.

14. Nietzsche, Friedrich. *Ecce Homo.* Trans. Duncun Large. New York: Oxford University Press. 2007. P. 14.

15. Nietzsche, Friedrich. *The Antichrist.* Trans. H. L. Mencken. New York: Alfred A. Knopf Inc., 1918. P. 10-11.

16. Ibid. p. 13.

17. Ibid. p. 10.

18. Nietzsche, Friedrich. *Beyond Good and Evil.* Trans. Walter Kaufmann. Vintage Books Edition. New York: Random House Inc., 1989. P. 20-21.

19. Nietzsche, Friedrich. *Thus Spoke Zarathustra.* Trans. Walter Kaufmann. Modern Library edition. New York: Random House USA, 1995. P. 34-35.

20. Nietzsche, Friedrich. *Beyond Good and Evil.* Trans. Walter Kaufmann. Vintage Books Edition. New York: Random House Inc., 1989. P. 67.

21. Ibid. p. 47.

22. Nietzsche, Friedrich. *The Gay Science.* Trans. Walter Kaufmann. Vintage Books edition. New York: Random House Publication, 1974. P. 167.

23. Ibid. p. 76.

24. Nietzsche, Friedrich. *Selected Letters of Friedrich Nietzsche.* Ed. Christopher Middleton. Indianapolis: Hackett Publishing Company, Inc., 1918. P. 282.

25. Peffers, Rose. *Nietzsche: The Disciple of Dionysus.* New Jersey: Associated University Presses, Inc., 1972. P. 79.

✳✳✳

Chapter 5

Concluding Nietzsche's Philosophy of religion: A destructive tool towards a constructive outlook

While concluding this research work, I find it mandatory to clear this in the very beginning that what I present here is not 'Nietzsche's philosophy of religion', rather; I am using 'Nietzsche's philosophy of religion' as a destructive tool to acquire a better perspective of religion, which was the purpose of this research work. My aim was to show how Nietzsche pokes holes in the well decorated curtains of social and religious culture, and exposes their hypocrisy and absurdity. Once one breaks through the glorified greatness of the concept, against which no one is allowed to raise questions, one can examine the worth of religion as I proposed when I started this work.

While starting my research work I had a vague idea of how I will deal with my topic, and I have worked in more or less same manner. In have started my work by introducing Friedrich Nietzsche as a dynamic philosopher who is far more relevant today than he was ever. The reason behind his gradual popularity is his straightforwardness and pragmatic life-affirming attitude. It is mandatory that we see now that due do the natural process of evolution there surfaces a new mass of people; a kind which is not ignorant enough as previous generations, so as to NOT notice the obvious contradictions of religious ways, which is not obedient enough to follow even though they see the contradictions. Neither is it enlightened enough to grasp the mystery of cosmos. We are now faced with a generation which would not settle for rigid traditions based on fictional theories; neither do they have time to long for larger than life

171

truths. This is the mass which is most influenced by Nietzsche. These are the people of whom the new world is composed of. Nietzsche's philosophy gives voice to their discomfort and repulsion generated by the conventional ideas of religion and morality. He speaks against the bias towards 'immediate certainties' and 'final truths' and asks to embrace life as it is, which all its joy and suffering. He invites thinkers to today to challenge the commonly accepted ideas in philosophy as well as in society. Instead of seeking refuge in superficial theories of religion which promises otherworldly solutions, he asks men to rejoice in the face of death and suffering. This is his Dionysian method, which he uses as a tool to overcome the fears responsible of religious dependency.

After providing a brief yet sufficient description of major philosophical insights of Friedrich Nietzsche, including his view regarding religion, I have objectively presented the need of philosophical examination of 'religion'. It is a well known yet least accepted fact that 'religion' has grown to become one of the major reasons of hatred, violence and 'mass-murder'. It is problem that needs to be acknowledged and dealt with. But first it is necessary to free ourselves from the prejudices that we carry as tradition and look deep into the history of religions in a disengaged manner. That is what I have done in my second chapter and I found that there are two parallel ideas associated with the term 'religion' that have been confused together since the beginning. One is of a unified vital force of which everything consists of about which physicists are continuously trying to comprehend more and more everyday and it keeps surprising them. Ancient religions honoured this force by honouring life and nature surrounding them by calling it

'Supreme God'. Physicists like Einstein, Carl Sagan and Stephen Hawking have time and again tried to underline the parallels between the cosmos and this 'supreme God'. 'Tao', 'Brahman', 'Ultimate', 'Universe' or 'Cosmos' seem to be same concept called by various names, understood in various forms.

Second idea, is of a 'personal God' that varies from religion to religion. It involves himself in petty human affairs. Gives order, expects loyalty, demands obedience, gets angry, punishes people even destroys them when disobeyed. He demands sacrifices, gets jealous, induces fear and takes revenge. In short, he does everything expected of a powerful but narcissist self centred king. He sends a rule-book for 'his' people and a religion is developed out of that rulebook. Now, this is the 'religion' responsible for every unfortunate event in the history of humanity. This is the religion against which Nietzsche and every other thinker who calls himself an 'atheist' has waged a war. This is the religion which breeds brainwashed mobs and from which individual needs to be protected.

Richard Dawkins's following illustration regarding the matter is noteworthy. He mentions the difference between the two contradictory understandings of the term 'God' which has created serious misunderstanding. One he calls 'supernatural religion' or 'supernatural God', other he calls by many names, one of which is Einsteinian Religion'. He says –

"By 'religion' Einstein meant something entirely different from what is conventionally meant. As I continue to clarify the distinction between supernatural religion on the one hand and Einsteinian religion

on the other, bear in mind that I am calling only supernatural gods delusional." (Dawkins 15)[1]

He further quotes Einstein to provide a glimpse of Einsteinian religion –

"*I have never imputed to Nature a purpose or a goal, or anything that could be understood as anthropomorphic. What I see in nature is a magnificent structure that we can comprehend only very imperfectly, and that must fill a thinking person with a feeling of humility. This is a genuinely religious feeling that has nothing to do with mysticism.*

The idea of a personal God is quite alien to me and seems even naive." (Dawkins 15)[2]

On the arbitrary use of term God Dawkins quotes Einstein and Carl Sagan –

"*Let me sum up the Einsteinium religion in one more quotation from Einstein himself: 'To sense that behind everything that can be experienced there is a something that our minds cannot grasp and whose beauty and sublimity reaches us only indirectly and as a feeble reflection, this is religiousness. In this sense I am religious.' In this sense I too am religious, with the reservation that 'cannot grasp' doesn't have to mean 'forever ungraspable'. But I prefer not to call myself religious because it is misleading. It is destructively misleading because, for the vast majority of people, 'religion' implies 'supernatural'. Carl Sagan put it well: '...if by "God" one means the set of physical laws that govern the universe, then clearly there is such God. This God is emotionally unsatisfying... it does not make much sense to pray to the law of gravity.'*

...Nevertheless, I wish that physicists would refrain from using the word God in their special metaphorical sense. The metaphorical or pantheistic God of the physicists is light years away from the interventionist, miracle wrecking, thought-reading, sin-punishing, prayer-answering God of the Bible, of priests, mullahs and rabbis, and of ordinary language. Deliberately to confuse the two is in my opinion, an act of intellectual high treason." (Dawkins 19)[3]

Although Dawkins calls it intellectual high treason for a physicist to use the term God in Einsteinian sense, for a philosopher it becomes an urgency to present this aspect of religion before the 'majority of people'. We need to present before them the laws of cosmos as they are, separated from their religious explanations. And we need to show them the absurdity of their beliefs again and again until it strikes them that there are other ways to look at the world, without the stained glass of religion.

In the chapter 'The collapse of God', I have very objectively presented the facts about the destruction caused by organised religions and the extent of the poisonous environment they could create. It's transparent that organised religions have failed in their purpose of 'binding the society', promoting love and brotherhood or the least, maintaining harmony. As a solution I have proposed an 'existential approach towards religion'. Though the phrase sound confusing, I have explained what it means and how it may be the only way we can find balance in the changing world. However it is important to mention that 'Existentialist approach' does not mean the same as Existentialism. An 'Existentialist approach' presupposes as a fundamental fact that one is not supposed to 'follow' a specific set of ideologies, instead it is applied as a second or third person to understand other's individuality in addition to one's own. It's not an entirely new idea, instead what I mean by the existential approach towards religion is the cliché ideology of 'live and let live'. The difference lies in the fact that existentialism expects one to 'live consciously'. I have gone through both; the theist and atheist existentialism and found that they both provide a way of living without interference of religious authorities and institutions. One wants to lead his life believing in God or he does not, it is entirely up to that particular individual, and 'I' as a second or third person to them will not impose on them my opinion regarding 'God', for example, Kierkegaard talks of a personal relationship with God, and Nietzsche ridicules worshipping 'pure forms', both are associated with existentialism, but one with an 'existentialist approach' need to agree with either of them, while respecting both.

Further, after analyzing Nietzsche's objections towards religion and examining the take of existentialists like Sartre, Kierkegaard and Camus, in the light of the destruction and toxic environment caused by organised religions in last few decades, I have found that though 'religion' and 'God' are an undeniable psychological necessity in the face of this vast 'nothingness' in order to survive, but those who claim authority over these religions demand a price too high, which I am afraid humanity won't be able to pay anymore. 'God', in the image of man, has been corrupted by manly errors and has lost its relevance. And the other God, the 'Einsteinian God', cannot be reduced within the limits of a specific religion.

But, common people are not strong enough to take responsibility of their own actions. The fear of death and non-existence is too strong to overcome hence the masses will eventually lean towards whatever support they can find. Therefore, we cannot snatch away their religion from them just yet, as it will lead to either chaos or nihilism. We have to let them grow with their own pace. Until then we have to find a method by which men can co-exist in harmony with their different faiths. Existentialist approach, as discussed before can serve as that method.

Also, in order to lead a life of quality, people need to break free from the possession of religion and develop acceptance and tolerance. Each of us has to leave 'extremism' and a find a more suitable way which would allow men to live with their dignity. There is a mixed racial world ahead of us, without sharp distinctions between the communities like tribal times, so we have to leave our tribal mentalities behind us. As we are evolving, we don't need a few things anymore, like long sharp nails, an appendix or an earlobe, 'tribal ego' is one of them! World is now small, every race is everywhere and we have to now grow out of our religious insecurities. The fear of becoming extinct! We are trying to hold really tight to our old values and traditions and yes they were beautiful, but those traditions were not here forever and neither is us.

When someone is born in a specific religion, he/she is not answerable to everything that has happened in that religion since it came into existence. A person might belong to a religion but that is not his only identity. Religion is one of an individual's many aspects. An individual has multiple dimensions, a Hindu, a Jew or a Muslim is not just a Hindu or Jew or a Muslim. He is a father, a son a pet-owner, music lover, employee, voter, tax-payer and a friend. He might be a liberal, atheist, not-so-religious, mystic, a spiritual or an orthodox. Every person has different roles and priorities. Adapting this individualistic approach might help people to understand that the person in front of or right next to you in NOT YOU. People have different experiences in life and different (sometimes polar opposite) opinions. Everyone has to understand that they cannot force their opinions and faith to other individual, whether the person is of other community/faith, their own community/faith, their own family of their own child. An individual may be influenced or convinced but he can never be forced to think a certain way. One cannot terrorize people to a have a certain faith. Faith cannot be induced by terror, violence or abuse. Problem arises when people are treated as sheep or rats! Not every individual can be shepherded that way, some are aware of who they are.

We can learn this from a group of friends whom we can find in every school and every college. How individuals with very different backgrounds come together with their individual dignities. How are they able to overlook the difference, how are they able to love a friend regardless his/her religion/race/community, how are they able to fall in love with a partner of different religion/race/community and spend whole life in togetherness, while their elder can't even digest the idea? Why is it that elderly and intellectuals are not able to find a solution regarding the matters of which kids and youth already have a solution? Even if one can't make the change overnight, the least one can do is to spare the children, and surprisingly, they won't even have to teach them NOT to be a 'racist'. They already are 'not racist', they don't discriminate we teach them so. We just have to keep our poison to ourselves and after the generations that are damaged beyond recovery pass away, we would have a chance at a better world.

The fact is, solution is always there, the 'problem' is a giant imaginary bubble of 'ego'/ 'pride', and when people look at things through it things seem distorted. All we need is a sharp idea to 'prick the bubble'. It's not even a new idea, as I have already said, it is the cliché idea of 'live and let live'. Now is the time to use it! 'prick the bubble'.

Citation and Reference :

1. Dawkins, Richard. *The God Delusion.* New delhi: Random House Publishers, 2006. P. 15.
2. Ibid.
3. Ibid. p. 19.

CPSIA information can be obtained
at www.ICGtesting.com
Printed in the USA
BVHW060857140123
656278BV00011B/1451

9 781805 454083